ROYAL NATIONAL THEATRE
COOKERY BOOK

ROYAL NATIONAL THEATRE
COOKERY BOOK

Recipes by **Melvin Schnable**
Introduction by **John Mortimer**

ABSOLUTE PRESS

Consultant **Barry Rushmer**

Book Designer **Michael Mayhew**

Editor **Lyn Haill**
Assistant Editor **Liz Curry**

With thanks to **Diane Benjamin** and **Laura Bishop** for their invaluable work
in obtaining permissions, to **Giles Croft** and **Alex Wilbraham** for help in
selecting quotations, and to **Anthony Smit** for graphic design assistance.

First Published by Absolute Press 14 Widcombe Crescent Bath England
and The Royal National Theatre South Bank London England

©Recipes: Melvin Schnable 1991
©Play Extracts: The Authors and Translators
©Introduction: John Mortimer 1991

Printed by Longdunn Press Ltd Barton Manor Bristol
Bound by The Bath Press Lower Bristol Road Bath

ISBN 0 948230 48 7

pickled herrings may have existed, or merely been a fictional excuse for the explosive sounds from which he took his name. Cakes, with ale on the side, however, were among the delights threatened by Malvolio. Illyrian cakes must have been something quite special, but once again the author fails to give us either the ingredients or the method. Christopher Sly in *The Taming of the Shrew* places an order for "conserves of beef" and Women's Institutes up and down the country have no doubt wondered how to turn a rump steak into a prize-winning jam; but it appears that Sly had no idea of what the word 'conserve' meant, and an interesting culinary idea is unexplained.

One of Shakespeare's most enticing meals, laid temptingly out in *The Tempest*, is made to vanish "with a quaint device" by the old Magician who is no doubt the author himself. This may lead us to believe that Shakespeare would never have appeared in the glossy magazines' lists of 'Foodies'. 'Drinkies' might have been a different matter. *Hamlet* is awash with alcohol from the moment Claudius downs his Rhenish to a ten gun salute until the poisoned loving cup. Iago ruins Cassio with a craftily placed offer of a quick one and *Antony and Cleopatra* seems to be a play about intoxication by love and wine. "Plumpy Bacchus with pink eyne" gets a far bigger part in the Shakespeare cannon than any emaciated and bearded chef painting abstracts on octagonal plates.

Our greatest dramatist may have avoided long and luxurious meals on stage because it's extremely hard to speak blank verse with your mouth full of roast ptarmigan stuffed with quails and oysters, or whatever was the high peak of Tudor gastronomy. His scenes are too short, too action packed, indeed too dramatic to allow for leisurely dining. Now and again attendants may rush on with gold painted goblets and platters, but they are usually empty and simulated mastication occupies the position of simulated sex in modern television drama. On the telly, of course, people are eating all the time. Meals have the great advantage of getting the characters sitting down in one position, so they can have a long conversation without the director having to think out elaborate camera movements. It's not possible to avoid such scenes entirely, but the truth of the matter is that few actors look good while eating and there are a number who find it impossible to remember lines and deal attractively with a plate of spaghetti. To play an eating scene requires considerably more technical skill than duelling with rapier and dagger or frothing at the mouth in a fit of jealous rage. Few of us who saw it will ever forget the technical brilliance of Sir Michael Hordern in Sheridan's *The Rivals*, who managed to deliver a flood of dialogue whilst actively consuming a boiled egg and toast soldiers. For once the dramatist, the actor and the food worked together in perfect harmony. As a general rule it has to be said that it's difficult to play tragedy while eating. "I can't eat muffins in an agitated manner," said Algernon in *The Importance of Being Earnest*. "The butter would probably get on my cuffs."

It can't be long before some director, desperate to put his mark on *Hamlet*, has the Prince contemplate self slaughter whilst dealing with a take-away kebab. I don't believe there is any up and coming actor sufficiently skilful to make a success of it.

It is now a heart-warming experience to come through the doors of the National Theatre. There is an infectious excitement, a shared anticipation of pleasure, in the foyers. *Ovations* is clearly part of that pleasure. In the old days I have taken the restaurant to task for not providing fish and chips, boiled beef and dumplings, steak and kidney pudding, which would, I think, be an excellent accompaniment to great British drama. Since then I have enjoyed many meals there, served with great courtesy and speed and it's good to have these recipes. You could all attempt them, but I warn you not to try acting whilst you're eating them, unless you happen to be Sir Michael Hordern.

THE LADY FROM MAXIMS
by GEORGES FEYDEAU
TRANSLATED BY JOHN MORTIMER

LYTTELTON 18 OCTOBER 1977,
DIRECTOR CHRISTOPHER MORAHAN
ETIENNE JOHN NORMINGTON,
DR PETYPON STEPHEN MOORE

ETIENNE Would M'sieur like luncheon...? We have liver pâté and a nice fat roast goose.

PETYPON (jumps) Uggh! Eating! Disgusting habit.

STARTERS

AVOCADO, MOZZARELLA AND TOMATO SALAD

Serves 4

1 large ripe avocado pear
1 lb (450g) plum tomatoes
4 oz (125g) mozzarella

For the dressing

2 tablespoons olive oil
1 tablespoon white wine vinegar
1 teaspoon Dijon mustard
half tablespoon chopped basil
salt
ground pepper
half tablespoon lemon juice
basil leaves for garnish

Wash tomatoes, de-stalk and slice thinly lengthways. Thinly slice mozzarella cheese. Quarter, peel and fan slice lengthways the avocado pear. Brush pear slices with lemon juice. In a bowl mix mustard and white wine vinegar and chopped basil, blend in the olive oil, and add salt and pepper to taste.

At top of plate arrange alternate slices of tomato and mozzarella cheese. Place the fanned avocado slices beneath and sprinkle basil dressing over the middle. Garnish with fresh basil leaf.

PLENTY
by **David Hare**
Lyttelton 12 April 1978,
Director **David Hare**
Susan Traherne **Kate Nelligan**

SUSAN Isn't this an exciting week? Don't you think? Isn't this thrilling? Everything up for grabs. At last. We will see some changes. Thank the Lord. Now, there was dinner. I made some more dinner for Leonard. A little ham. And chicken. And some pickles and tomato. And lettuce. And there are a couple of pheasants in the fridge. And I can get twelve bottles of claret from the cellar. Why not?

There is plenty.

Shall we eat again?

BABY SPINACH SALAD

Serves 4

12oz (350g) baby spinach
4 large rindless rashers streaky bacon
1 oz (25g) pine kernels
1 oz (25g) whole hazelnuts
1 slice white toast bread
oil for frying

For the dressing

1 tablespoon sunflower oil
1 tablespoon hazelnut oil
1 tablespoon champagne vinegar
1 small garlic clove crushed
salt
ground black pepper
1 teaspoon Dijon mustard

De-stalk and thoroughly wash and dry the spinach. Cut bacon into small squares and grill until crisp. De-crust the bread and cut remaining slice into half inch (1 cm) squares, fry in oil until golden brown, drain on absorbent paper.

Place pine kernels and hazelnuts under the grill and toast until brown.

In a bowl, mix mustard, garlic clove and champagne vinegar, then blend in both oils, add salt and pepper to taste.

Place spinach leaves in four separate bowls and sprinkle on equal quantities of cooled bacon, nuts and croutons. Coat each salad with dressing and serve immediately.

SAUTÉED WILD MUSHROOMS ON OAKLEAF SALAD

Serves 4

1lb (450g) selection of wild mushrooms in season
2 oz (50g) butter
2 oz (50g) shallots, peeled and finely chopped
1 tablespoon freshly chopped basil
half oakleaf lettuce (washed and dried)
salt
ground black pepper

Wipe mushrooms with damp cloth and slice larger mushrooms to provide even sizes. Melt butter in frying pan, add shallots and sauté until starting to brown. Add mushrooms to the pan and toss with shallots for a few minutes until cooked but still firm. Add chopped basil and seasoning, mix together and place on top of arranged oak-leaf lettuce. Serve immediately whilst still hot.

GRILLED GOAT'S CHEESE SALAD

Serves 4

4 thick slices cylindrical soft goat's cheese
1 oz (25g) sesame seeds
1 head radicchio (washed and dried)
half head curly endive (washed and dried)
1 oz (25g) toasted pine nuts

For the dressing

2 tablespoons olive oil
1 tablespoon white wine vinegar
½ garlic clove, crushed
1 tablespoon chopped chives
1 teaspoon grain mustard
salt
ground black pepper

Arrange on each plate a bed of radicchio and curly endive. In a bowl, mix the grain mustard, garlic and white wine vinegar, blend in the olive oil, the majority of chopped chives and salt and pepper to taste. Sprinkle over salad leaves.

Coat each slice of cheese with the sesame seeds, place under hot grill and toast until the seeds brown and the cheese softens slightly. Place on top of salad and sprinkle with pine nuts and remaining chopped chives. Serve immediately.

ROQUEFORT AND CELERIAC SALAD

Serves 4

6 oz (175g) Roquefort cheese, cubed
1 head celeriac
half head curly endive
1 lemon (squeezed)
4 oz (125g) chopped walnuts
1 tablespoon chopped fresh parsley

For the dressing

1 tablespoon walnut oil
1 tablespoon sunflower oil
1 tablespoon white wine vinegar
salt
ground black pepper

Peel and finely grate the celeriac, toss in lemon juice to prevent discolouring and combine in large bowl with the curly endive.

Place the white wine vinegar in a bowl with salt and pepper and blend in both oils.

Divide the salad between four bowls and sprinkle equal amounts of Roquefort and chopped walnuts on each. Coat each salad with walnut dressing and garnish with chopped parsley.

BRESAOLA AND PARMESAN SALAD

Serves 4

2 oz (50g) Bresaola (air-cured beef), thinly sliced
2 oz (50g) fresh Parmesan, thinly sliced
half head curly endive
juice of one lemon
1 fl oz (25ml) olive oil
ground black pepper

Place a bed of curly endive on each plate and, on top, place alternate layers of Bresaola and Parmesan. Mix the olive oil, lemon juice and black pepper and sprinkle over. Serve immediately

CHILLED WHITE GAZPACHO

Serves 4

3 oz (75g) white ground almonds
10 oz (275g) fresh white breadcrumbs
2 large garlic cloves
1 egg
6 fl oz (175ml) olive oil
3 fl oz (75ml) sherry wine vinegar
2 pints (1.14 lts) water
12 seedless white grapes (halved)
1 tablespoon chopped parsley
salt

Place the egg and garlic cloves in a food processor and blend well. Add the breadcrumbs, ground almonds and one pint of water, process until a smooth paste. Gradually add the olive oil and vinegar in a thin stream until mixed. Add salt and taste for seasoning.

Transfer the mixture to a large non-metallic bowl and add remaining water until desired consistency is achieved. Cover the soup and chill for 3-4 hours.

Ladle into soup cups and garnish with grapes. Sprinkle with chopped parsley.

15

COVENT GARDEN SOUP

Serves 4

2 oz (50g) of each of the following vegetables, all finely chopped:
onion
celery
carrot
courgette
leek
cauliflower
potato
haricots verts
broccoli
fennel
4 oz (125g) butter
2 pints (1.14 lts) water
salt
ground black pepper
½ tablespoon chopped chervil
½ tablespoon chopped chives

Melt the butter in a pan, add vegetables and cook without browning over low heat for a few minutes to extract flavour. Add two pints of water, lightly season, bring to boil and skim. Reduce heat and simmer gently for 15 minutes until vegetables are tender.

To serve, place in individual bowls and sprinkle with chopped chervil and chives.

MA RAINEY'S BLACK BOTTOM
by **August Wilson**
Cottesloe 25 October 1989,
Director **Howard Davies**
Toledo **Clarke Peters**

TOLEDO Now I'm gonna show you how this goes ... where you just a leftover from history. Everybody come from different places in Africa right? Come from different tribes and things. Sonnawhile they begin to make one big stew. You had the carrots, the peas, and potatoes and what not over here. And over there, you had the meat, the nuts, the okra, corn ... and then you mix it up and let it cook right through to get the flavors flowing together ... then you got one thing. You got a stew. Now you take and eat the stew. You take and make your history with that stew. All right. Now it's over. Your history's over and you done ate the stew. But you look around and you see some carrots over here, some potatoes over there. That stew's still there. You done made your history and it's still there. You can't eat it all. So what you got? You got some leftovers. That's what it is. You got some leftovers and you can't do nothing with it. You already making you another history ... cooking you another meal, and you don't need them leftovers no more. What to do. See, we's the leftovers. The colored man is the leftovers.

16

CREAM OF SORREL SOUP

A PLACE WITH THE PIGS
by **Athol Fugard**
Cottesloe 16 February 1988,
Director **Athol Fugard**
Praskovya **Linda Bassett,**
Pavel **Jim Broadbent**

Serves 4

2 oz (50g) butter
1 medium onion, chopped
1 white part of leek, chopped
1 celery stalk, chopped
1 medium carrot, chopped
2lb (900g) sorrel leaves
2 pints (1.14 lts) vegetable
stock
salt
ground black pepper
4 fl oz (125 ml) sour cream
1 tablespoon chopped chives

Melt butter in a pan and, over a low heat, add onion, leek, celery and carrots and lightly cook, covered, for 10 minutes. Place to one side.

Boil 4 fl oz (125 ml) of water and add sorrel leaves, cook over a high heat for 3-5 minutes, then add to other pan of vegetables. Add the vegetable stock, bring to boil and simmer until vegetables will purée. Strain, reserving the stock, and process until puréed.

Combine purée with stock in a pan, season to taste and serve topped with sour cream and chopped chives.

PRASKOVYA Pavel ... I don't mean to interrupt but ... can I ask a question?

(No response from PAVEL)

What immediate effect does all of that have on things ... and the situation in here ... What I mean is ... I don't want to interfere but it.is getting on for supper time and well ... must I go on with it ... or what?

(No response)

Pavel?

PAVEL (violently) I heard you.

(Another pause)

PRASKOVYA Well?

PAVEL (it is not easy for him) Have we got a little aniseed for the dumplings?

PRASKOVYA Yes.

PAVEL Soup and dumplings.

CONTENTS

Food in the Theatre
by John Mortimer

"Gall of goat and slips of yew
Sliver'd in the moon's eclipse
Nose of Turk and Tartar's lips..."

This is the nearest Shakespeare comes to a recipe. The witches give us the ingredients in some detail and they can easily be imagined appearing on television and saying, "And here's a tiger's chawdron that I prepared earlier". As a rule this author gives us few ideas for an easy to prepare banquet for fifty. The Capulets threw such a party, but all we are told is that they served march pane, some of which the waiters kept to themselves. Anyone who could write a stage direction like "enter a server and divers servants with dishes and services, over the stage" without telling whether these divers dishes were marinated, pot roasted or stir fried would hardly be given space in the Sunday supplements. What did the Macbeths have for dinner, apart from an unexpected visit from Banquo's ghost? I know what they didn't have. I don't suppose they sat down to a small portion of monkfish arranged on an octagonal plate with a single black olive, a smear of pink sauce and a sprig of dill to pose as a main course. Life might have been draughty or dangerous during weekends with the Macbeths at Dunsinane Castle, but you were at least spared the horrors of 'nouvelle cuisine'. You gnawed your way through large slabs of rare venison and half a dozen grouse before the huge pies with crusts shaped like battlements gave you a sleepless night.

Shakespeare can't be counted as a great food writer. Funeral bakemeats are reported in *Hamlet* but no recipe is given. I imagine they must have been rather like those 'cold collations' left out by landladies for the actors when they came home late after the show. Corned beef figured, I should think, and that horrible shiny supermarket ham, and half a Scotch egg if you were lucky, coldly furnished forth the table. Toby Belch's

FENNEL SOUP

Serves 4

1½ lbs (700g) fennel
4 oz (125g) onion, finely
chopped
3 oz (75g) butter
2 pints (1.14 lts) vegetable
stock
salt
ground black pepper
1 slice toast bread
2 oz (50g) Bel Paese cheese

Cut off the fennel ferns and reserve for garnish. Finely slice the remaining fennel bulbs. Melt 2 oz (50g) of the butter in a pan, add the chopped onion and lightly cook over a low heat. Add to the pan the sliced fennel and sweat for a further ten minutes. Add two pints of vegetable stock, bring to boil, skim and simmer until tender.

De-crust the bread and cut into half inch (1 cm) squares and fry in the remaining butter until golden brown. Drain on absorbent paper.

Dice the Bel Paese cheese. To serve, place in individual bowls, sprinkle with diced cheese and croutons, garnish with fennel ferns.

SHRIMP BISQUE

Serves 4

8 oz (225g) pink shrimps
2 oz (50g) tomato purée
5 tablespoons dry white wine
5 tablespoons brandy
½ tablespoon chopped dill
1 garlic clove, crushed
1 bay leaf
1 sprig thyme
3 oz (75g) onion, chopped
3 oz (75g) carrot, chopped
3 oz (75g) celery, chopped
5 fl oz (150ml) double cream
3 oz (75g) butter
1½ oz (40g) plain flour
2 pints (1.14 lts) fish stock
salt
ground black pepper
cayenne pepper

Melt half the butter in a pan, add the onion, carrot, celery and garlic and lightly cook till vegetables soften. Add the shrimps, bay leaf, thyme and a pinch of cayenne pepper. Raise the heat, add the brandy and white wine, add to this the tomato purée.

Pour in the fish stock, bring to boil, skim, and simmer for 45 minutes. Strain, reserving the fluid, and purée the ingredients in the blender. Combine with the reserved fluid.

In another pan melt the remaining butter, add flour, stir and cook for one and a half minutes, remove from the heat. Slowly add the liquid mixture to the roux and stir constantly. Simmer for a further 20 minutes on low heat stirring occasionally to prevent sticking. Strain through a fine sieve, adjust seasoning.

Place in serving bowls, swirl in double cream and garnish with chopped dill.

BROCCOLI MOUSSE

Serves 4

4 oz (125g) broccoli heads, chopped
3 fl oz (75ml) vegetable velouté
¼ oz (5g) powdered gelatine
2 tablespoons vegetable stock
salt
ground white pepper
3 fl oz (75ml) whipped cream
1 oz (25g) chopped shallots
½ oz (10g) butter
4 shelled walnuts
4 sprigs chervil
walnut oil mayonnaise to serve

Melt the butter in a pan, add the shallots and cook till transparent. Add broccoli and cook for a few minutes until tender and any liquor has reduced. Cool and place in blender with vegetable velouté and purée. Soften the gelatine in a little cold water, add to hot vegetable stock until dissolved. Add this to the broccoli purée, adjust seasoning. Allow to cool slightly.

Before mixture begins to set add a quarter of the whipped cream. Allow to cool more, then fold in rest of whipped cream. Place into moulds and leave to set in refrigerator.

Remove from moulds and serve with mayonnaise made with walnut oil. Garnish with half shelled walnut and sprig of chervil.

BASIC VELOUTÉ SAUCE

To make ½ pint (300 ml):

3oz (75g) butter
3oz (75g) flour
½ pint stock (use vegetable, white veal, chicken or fish according to flavour required)

Melt the butter slowly in a heavy saucepan. When it has just melted, draw the pan off the heat and add the sifted flour. Stir until the mixture is smooth, this is called a roux. Cook the roux in a cool oven, Gas mark 2 (300°F) (150°C) until the texture is sandy. Make sure not to colour the roux. Put back on the heat, and add the stock, stirring constantly. Bring to the boil and continue cooking slowly for another 30 minutes. Only season very slightly.

As soon as the velouté is cooked remove all fat and strain into a bowl. Butter the top to prevent a skin forming. Use as desired.

MAYONNAISE

Serves 6

3-4 egg yolks
1 pint (600 ml) olive oil at room temperature
salt
pepper
1 tablespoon vinegar
1 teaspoon English mustard

Stir the egg yolks with a whisk in a bowl with salt, pepper, mustard and half the vinegar. Add the oil drop by drop, then in a very thin stream as the sauce begins to bind, stirring vigorously. Add a few drops of vinegar from time to time, together with the oil. Then add the remainder of the vinegar and continue to stir until all the oil has been used and the sauce is thick and smooth. To make Walnut Mayonnaise simply substitute Walnut oil for Olive oil.

WAITING FOR GODOT

by **Samuel Beckett**
Lyttelton 25 November 1987
Director **Michael Rudman**
Estragon **John Alderton,**
Vladimir **Alec McCowen**

ESTRAGON (violently) I'm hungry.

VLADIMIR Do you want a carrot?

ESTRAGON Is that all there is?

VLADIMIR I might have some turnips.

ESTRAGON Give me a carrot. (VLADIMIR rummages in his pockets, takes out a turnip and gives it to ESTRAGON. Angrily) It's a turnip. (VLADIMIR moves away)

VLADIMIR Oh pardon! I could have sworn it was a carrot. (He rummages again in his pockets, finds nothing but turnips) All that's turnips. (He rummages) Wait, I have it. (He brings out a carrot, goes to ESTRAGON and gives it to him) There, dear fellow. (VLADIMIR moves away. ESTRAGON begins to eat the carrot) Give me the turnip. (He goes to ESTRAGON. ESTRAGON gives back the turnip which VLADIMIR puts in his pocket and moves away) Make it last, that's the end of them.

CARROT MOUSSE

Serves 4

4 oz (125g) carrots
3 fl oz (75ml) vegetable velouté (see page 21)
¼ oz (5g) powdered gelatine
2 tablespoons vegetable stock
salt
½ teaspoon sugar
ground white pepper
3 fl oz (75ml) whipped cream
1 oz (25g) chopped shallots
½ oz (10g) butter
2 fl oz (50ml) sour cream
½ tablespoon snipped chives
4 sprigs flat parsley

Melt the butter in a pan, add the shallots and cook until transparent. Add the carrots (reserving a few slices for garnish) and sugar, and cook for a few minutes until tender and any liquor has been reduced. Cool and place in blender with vegetable velouté and purée.

Soften the gelatine in a little cold water and add to hot vegetable stock until dissolved. Add this to the carrot purée, adjust seasoning. Allow to cool slightly.

Before mixture begins to set add a quarter of the whipped cream. Allow to cool further, then fold in the rest of the whipped cream. Place into moulds and leave to set in refrigerator.

Remove from moulds and serve with sour cream and snipped chives. Garnish with a slice of blanched fluted carrot and flat parsley.

Mange-Tout Soufflé

Serves 4

1lb (450g) mange-tout,
trimmed
1 dessertspoon spring onion,
finely chopped
½ oz (10g) gelatine
pinch sugar
salt
ground black pepper
1 lemon, squeezed
8 fl oz (225ml) whipping
cream
2 egg whites, stiffly beaten
½ pint (275ml) water
Melba toast to serve

Set aside 8 blanched mange-tout in a pan with the chopped spring onion. Add to this pan nearly ½ pint (275ml) of boiling water leaving enough to dissolve gelatine. Cook the mange-tout until just tender and liquidize the contents of the pan. Pass mixture through a fine sieve. This should leave approximately ¾ pint (400ml) of mixture.

Dissolve the gelatine in the remaining warm water and add to the purée. Adjust seasoning and add lemon juice. Allow to cool in refrigerator. Whip cream until softly stiff and fold into purée when about to set, followed by the beaten egg white.

Place paper collars on 4 ramekins and pour mixture in, to half inch above lip of dish. Leave to set firmly for several hours in refrigerator.

To serve, remove paper collars, place on plate and garnish with blanched mange-tout. Serve with melba toast.

TOMATO AND BASIL MOUSSE

Serves 4

6 oz (175g) tomatoes, peeled,
seeded and diced
1½ tablespoons tomato ketchup
1 tablespoon tomato juice
2 tablespoons tomato purée
salt
sugar
cayenne pepper
¼ oz (5g) gelatine powder
2 tablespoons hot vegetable
stock
5 fl oz (150ml) whipped cream
½ tablespoon basil, chopped

Strain half the tomato flesh through a fine sieve, add the tomato ketchup, juice and purée, season with salt, sugar and cayenne pepper. Soften the gelatine in the vegetable stock. Whisk into the tomato mixture with the chopped basil.

Before the mixture sets, whisk in a quarter of the whipped cream. Allow to cool, then fold in remaining cream with wooden spoon. Add remaining tomato flesh and when almost set, place into moulds. Chill in refrigerator till set.

Remove mousse from moulds onto plate and surround with avocado sauce. Serve with Melba toast.

AVOCADO SAUCE

½ pint (300 ml) mayonnaise
(see recipe 12)
1 large ripe avocado
1 tablespoon lemon juice
salt
pepper

Cut the avocado in half and discard the stone. Scoop out all the flesh into a glass bowl. Add the lemon juice, salt and pepper and mix to a fine purée. Now fold in the mayonnaise and mix to a smooth texture.

Wild Mushroom Terrine

Serves 4

1 teaspoon olive oil
10 oz (275g) wild mushrooms,
cleaned and sliced
1 oz (25g) lean chicken breast
1 oz (25g) lean veal topside
salt
ground black pepper
2 fl oz (50ml) double cream
½ teaspoon chopped chervil
½ teaspoon chopped parsley
1 sprig fresh thyme
1 oz (25g) shallots, finely
chopped
½ garlic clove, finely chopped
4 fl oz (125ml) tomato coulis -
(see page 55)

Heat oil in pan and fry mushrooms over a high heat for a few minutes, add the shallots, garlic and herbs. Reduce heat and cook for a further minute. Allow to cool and leave to marinate overnight.

Place chicken, veal, salt and pepper in processor and blend till fine. Chill until cold then add cold cream to processor to make a smooth mixture. Transfer to a stainless steel bowl and mix together with marinated mushrooms.

Grease a 1 pint (570ml) terrine mould and fill with mixture, cover with buttered greaseproof paper. Place terrine mould in bain-marie and cook in a cool oven, gas mark 2 (300°f) (150°c) for 25–30 minutes. Remove from oven and allow to cool. Remove from terrine and slice, serve with tomato coulis and crusty French bread.

IN HIS OWN WRITE
by **John Lennon**
Old Vic 18 June 1968,
Director **Victor Spinetti**
Sherlock Womlbs **Kenneth Mackintosh**

WOMLBS Now my dear Whopper, back to Bugger Street for a gottle of geer, three eggs with little liars on, two rashers of bacon, a bowl of Rice Krustchovs, a fresh grapeful, mushrides, some freed tomorrows, a basket of fruits and a cup of teens.

WATERCRESS MOUSSE

Serves 4

8 oz (225g) watercress
5 fl oz (150ml) double cream
3 large eggs
½ garlic clove, finely chopped
pinch ground black pepper
pinch nutmeg, grated

For the sauce

1 oz (25g) butter
1 small carrot finely cut in strips
1 small celery stalk finely cut in strips
half a small leek(white only), finely cut in strips
2 fl oz (50ml) vegetable stock
2 fl oz (50ml) dry white wine
2 fl oz (50ml) double cream
salt
ground black pepper

Wash the watercress, discard the stems and purée in liquidizer. Add the cream and blend. Transfer mixture to a bowl and whisk in the eggs one by one, add garlic, salt, pepper and nutmeg to taste.

Pour the mixture into 4 x 4 oz (125ml) buttered ramekins. Place in bain-marie and bake in pre-heated moderate oven, gas mark 4 (350°f) (180°c) for 30 minutes or until the mousse has risen and is golden in colour. Test by inserting knife into centre which should remove clean. Remove from bain-marie and place on a wire rack for 5 minutes.

To make sauce, sauté the carrot, celery and leek in the butter over a low heat till tender. Remove vegetables and place to one side. Add vegetable stock and white wine to pan and reduce to half original volume. Add the double cream and cook for a few minutes until sauce has slightly thickened. Return vegetables to the sauce. Season to taste. Remove mousse from ramekin, place on warm plate and surround with sauce..

THE WIND IN THE WILLOWS

by **Kenneth Grahame**
adapted by **Alan Bennett**
Olivier 12 December 1990,
Director **Nicholas Hytner**
Rat **Richard Briers**,
Mole **David Bamber**

RAT Listen, if you've nothing else on this morning what say we drop down the river together and make a day of it?

MOLE In the boat? Together? Could we? Could we really?

RAT Certainly. Hop in. Careful. Splendid.

(He gets a hamper)

Put this on your lap.

MOLE What's in it?

RAT Our lunch. There's cold chicken, cold ham, cold tongue, cold beef, pickled gherkin, sausage rolls, cress sandwiches, ginger beer, lemonade . . .

MOLE Oh stop, stop. This is too much.

RAT Do you really think so? It's only what I always take. The other animals are always saying I'm a mean beast, and cut it very fine.

BAKED POTTED CHEESE

Serves 4

¼ pint (150ml) thick Béchamel
sauce
8 oz (225g) Cheddar cheese,
grated
4 oz (125g) Emmenthal, grated
4 oz (125g) Gruyère, grated
1 fl oz (25ml) brandy
half tablespoon English
mustard, ready mixed
salt
ground black pepper
4 sprigs parsley
4 slices toast bread

Place into the hot Béchamel sauce each grated cheese, stirring continuously until fully melted. Add the brandy and English mustard, salt and pepper to taste and mix thoroughly until smooth consistency is achieved.

Place into four individual pots or ramekins, place in oven, gas mark 4 (350°f) (180°c) until browned. Toast the 4 slices of bread and cut into fingers. To serve, place cheese pots on napkined plate surrounded by toast fingers to dip. Garnish with parsley sprigs.

**BÉCHAMEL
(WHITE MILK SAUCE)**

To make ½ pint (300 ml):

3oz (75g) butter
3oz (75g) flour
½ pt (275 ml) milk

Make a roux with the butter and flour. Cook in a heavy saucepan for a few minutes over a gentle heat. Warm the milk and then add it to the roux, about a third at a time. Bring the sauce to boiling point, stirring all the time. The sauce should be cooked very gently to avoid burning. Season with salt and pepper. Strain. Coat with butter to prevent a skin from forming.

SPINACH, PRAWN AND MUSHROOM RAMEKINS

Serves 4

2 oz (50g) mushrooms, wiped and sliced
¼ pint (150ml) Béchamel sauce
½ oz (10g) butter
4 oz (125g) cooked spinach, drained and chopped
4 oz (125g) peeled prawns
salt
ground black pepper
2 oz (50g) grated Cheddar
4 parsley sprigs

Fry mushrooms in butter until soft, leave to cool. Make layers in each ramekin with the spinach, prawns, mushrooms and Béchamel finishing with the sauce, seasoning as you go. Sprinkle grated Cheddar on top, place in oven, gas mark 4 (350°f) (180°c) for approximately 10 minutes, brown under grill if necessary. Place ramekin in centre of plate and garnish with parsley sprigs.

HOT FISH TERRINE

Serves 4

6 oz (165g) whiting fillet
3 oz (75g) monkfish fillet
3 oz (75g) brill fillet
6 fl oz (175ml) double cream
1 large egg white
salt
ground white pepper
pinch saffron in teaspoon water
1 teaspoon chopped dill
1 dessertspoon puréed spinach

For garnish

½ oz (10g) red lumpfish roe
½ oz (10g) black lumpfish roe
4 sprigs dill

Purée the whiting, monkfish and brill fillets in the processor. With the machine running add the egg white until well blended and forms together. Pass the purée through a fine sieve into a stainless steel bowl and refrigerate for 30 minutes.

Place stainless steel bowl over bowl of crushed ice and slowly beat in double cream with wooden spoon, season to taste. Divide mixture into three bowls. Add saffron to one bowl, dill to the second and spinach to the third, and mix well.

Lightly butter and line a 1 pint (570ml) terrine mould with greaseproof paper. Place the mixture with dill into the terrine first and smooth down. Next add the the mixture with saffron and smooth down. Finally add the mixture with spinach. Top with buttered greaseproof and place in bain-marie with water half way up terrine mould. Cook in oven at gas mark 2 (300°f) (150°c) for approximately 30 minutes. Test by inserting skewer which should remove clean. When cooked, remove from oven, remove from terrine and slice.

GAME PÂTÉ EN CROÛTE

WHITE WINE & BUTTER SAUCE

1 oz (25g) shallots finely chopped
2 fl oz (50ml) dry white wine
2 fl oz (50ml) white wine vinegar
8 oz (225g) unsalted white butter (cubed)
salt
ground white pepper

To make the sauce, combine the shallots, white wine and vinegar in pan and simmer uncovered until the liquid has reduced to about 1 tablespoon. Over a low heat whisk in the butter one piece at a time, waiting for each piece to melt into the sauce. Continue until all the butter is used up, whisking constantly. Do not let the sauce get too hot or it will separate. The sauce should be a thick and creamy consistency. Season to taste. To serve, place a slice of hot terrine on each plate, surround with sauce, lumpfish roe and sprigs of dill.

Serves up to 20

12 oz (350g) lean venison
9 oz (250g) lean pork
2 teaspoons mixed game seasoning
1 teaspoon basil
½ teaspoon oregano
10 crushed juniper berries
2 garlic cloves, crushed
1 orange rind, grated
1½ teaspoons salt
2 small pork fillets
1 oz (25g) butter
1 oz (25g) shallots, diced
3 tablespoons gin
¼ pint (150ml) game stock
11 oz (300g) pork fat
1 tablespoon green peppercorns, chopped
4 oz (125g) ham, cooked and diced
1½ lb (700g) shortcrust pastry
1 egg yolk
5 fl oz (150ml) Madeira aspic
2 tablespoons oil
4 sprigs thyme
bayleaf
cranberry sauce

Cut the venison and lean pork into strips. Sprinkle with the seasoning and salt. Cover and leave to stand in refrigerator until needed.

Heat the oil in a pan and seal the trimmed pork fillets. Remove from the pan and pour off the oil, add the butter and lightly cook the shallots, stir in the gin and add the gamestock, garlic and juniper berries. Reduce by half, strain and reserve the liquid.

Mince the chilled meat through a fine plate. Cut the pork fat into strips and mince through same plate. Place the meat in a bowl over ice and work in the fat and reserved sauce. Add the chopped green peppercorns and work into the forcemeat with the diced ham. Cut the pork fillets into strips.

Line a 2¾ pint (1.5 lts) pâté tin with the pastry and ½ inch (1cm) layer of forcemeat, cover with strips of pork fillet, add another layer of forcemeat and press down well. Continue until all mixture has been used.

Cover the pâté with pastry, glaze with egg yolk and bake for 10 minutes at gas mark 9 (475°f) (240°c) then turn down to gas mark 6 (400°f) (200°c) and cook for a further 35 minutes. Remove from oven.

When cool, pour aspic through pastry holes on top of pâté. Place in fridge. To serve, place one slice on each plate garnished with cranberry sauce and sprigs of thyme and bayleaf.

Guinea Fowl Terrine with Sweetbreads and Morels

Serves 12

2¾ quarter pints (1.6 lts) veal stock
11 oz (300g) lean guinea fowl meat
3 oz (75g) crustless sliced white bread
1 egg white, lightly beaten
6 tablespoons single cream
¼ oz (5g) salt
ground white pepper
1 tablespoon chopped sage
1 tablespoon chopped rosemary
½ pint (275ml) whipped cream
1lb (450g) veal sweetbreads
1½ oz dried morel mushrooms
1 tablespoon chopped parsley
½ oz butter (10g)(for greasing)
Grape preserve for garnish

Cut the guinea fowl into strips and place on stainless steel tray. Arrange the sliced bread over the meat, moisten the bread with the egg white and single cream, add the salt, sage, rosemary, and pepper. Cover and chill.

When cold, mince the contents of tray twice through a fine plate. Place into a stainless steel bowl and work in the whipped cream a little at a time.

Soak the sweetbreads in running water and remove the skin and blood vessels to leave about 9 oz (250g) of flesh. Blanch in hot water, transfer to a saucepan with half the veal stock. Bring to boil and simmer for 10 minutes, leave to cool in stock. When cool, remove sweetbreads from the pan and cut into ½ inch (1cm) squares. Reduce the veal stock to a thick liquid and return sweetbreads to reduced stock. Remove contents from pan and chill.

Soak the morels in water, thoroughly wash away any sand, change water several times until they are completely swollen. Boil the morels in the remaining veal stock for 25 minutes then remove from pan. Reduce this stock to a thick liquid, pour over morels and chill.

Mix the sweetbreads and morels into the forcemeat, add the parsley.

Grease a 1¾ pint (1 ltr) terrine with butter and line with greaseproof paper. Fill with the forcemeat, smooth the top, removing any oil. Cover the top with greaseproof paper. Place in bain-marie and cook in moderate oven, gas mark 2 (300°f) (150°c) for 40 minutes. When cooked, cool, slice, and garnish with grape preserve.

THE ROMANS IN BRITAIN
by **Howard Brenton**
Olivier 16 October 1980,
Director **Michael Bogdanov**
First Cook **John Normington**,
Steward **Peter Needham**

1st COOK My family goes back a long way. To the kitchens of the Emperors of Rome.

There's a story in my family. One of us, a long time ago, served up an ox to an Emperor. Whole. "What?" cried the Emperor. "Cook an ox with the entrails and all the shit entire?" And my ancestor is dragged in on his knees. He begs a sword. But not for his throat. He slashes the ox's basted belly – and out tumble, why, chicken hearts, stewed larks, the tasty livers of little lambs. The kidneys of the ox drained of the blood and folded in the delicate flesh of marinated, white fish. All of it bound with butter, garlic, parsley and dry white wine.

The Imperial Ox! I've always wanted to cook it.

The trick is that with all that offal you don't need salt in the stuffing.

STEWARD Huh. Things being what they are, you're going to be out of a job.

1st COOK Yeah, I wonder what they're all eating out there, these days. S'pose I can go and cook for the Saxons. Human brains. Tricky, brain dishes.

GARLIC BAKED MUSHROOMS

Serves 4

12 large cup mushrooms
2 oz (50g) shallots, chopped
4 oz (125g) butter
1 oz (25g) garlic, chopped
4 oz (125g) fresh white
breadcrumbs
2 tablespoons chives, chopped
2 tablespoons parsley, chopped
2 tablespoons lemon juice
salt
ground black pepper
1 egg
2 oz (50g) freshly grated
Parmesan
2 fl oz (50ml) dry white wine
parsley to garnish

Wipe the mushrooms and remove stalks. Chop the stalks finely. Heat the butter in a pan and place cup mushrooms, round side down, in pan to brown. Remove from pan and set aside. Place the garlic, shallots, chopped stalks in the pan and cook for 2-3 minutes stirring continually.

Add lemon juice and wine and reduce till nearly evaporated. Remove from heat, add the breadcrumbs and herbs, adjust seasoning and bind with egg.

Spoon mixture into mushroom cups place on baking tray, sprinkle with Parmesan cheese and bake for 10 minutes on gas mark 4 (350°F) (180°c). Brown under grill. Place on plate and garnish with parsley.

Avocado Fan with Strawberry Vinaigrette

Serves 4

2 avocados
¼ pint (150ml) sunflower oil
4 oz (125g) fresh strawberries
2 fl oz (50ml) champagne
vinegar
sugar to taste
salt
ground white pepper
4 sprigs mint

Cut two strawberries in half and reserve for garnish. In a processor blend the remaining strawberries and oil till smooth. Season to taste with the champagne vinegar, sugar, salt and pepper.

Halve the avocados, peel and slice thinly lengthways, leaving ½ inch (1 cm) at the pointed end uncut. Press on to plate and fan out. Cover the uncut end with dressing, garnish with strawberry halves and mint leaves.

SPINACH GNOCCHI

Serves 4

1 pint (570 ml) milk
4 oz (125g) unsalted butter
1 tablespoon unsalted butter
8 oz (225g) semolina
3 oz (75g) fresh grated Parmesan
2 oz (50g) spinach, chopped and cooked
1 tablespoon grated Gruyère cheese
pinch salt
parsley to garnish

Bring the milk to the boil, stir in the salt and one tablespoon of butter, sprinkle the semolina into the boiling milk, stirring continually. Cook over a low heat for 20 minutes, stirring occasionally.

Remove from heat, add 1 tablespoon of Parmesan and the chopped spinach. Mix thoroughly. Pour onto a buttered tray, smooth out to quarter inch (0.5cm) thick. Allow to cool and solidify and cut into desired shapes with pastry cutter.

Place the gnocchi on buttered oven-proof dishes, and brush the shapes with butter. Sprinkle with the remaining Parmesan and Gruyère and bake in hot oven – Gas mark 6 (400°f) (200°c) – for 10 minutes or until browned. Serve immediately, garnished with chopped parsley.

THE NATIONAL HEALTH

by Peter Nichols
Old Vic 16 October 1969,
Director **Michael Blakemore**
Ash **Robert Lang**.

ASH That bed just happened
to fall vacant this morning.
Next to you on the other side

Desmond Foster, coronary.
Young for that, only forty. Then
me, Mervyn Ash, tummy ulcer.
Been here a fortnight so far.
On a blotting paper diet.
Tapioca, semolina, boiled fish,
chicken. The merest glimpse of
semolina makes me heave.
Always has. Don't ask me why.

TOMATO GNOCCHI

GRILLED SARDINES WITH GARLIC

Serves 6

5 oz (150g) freshly grated
Parmesan
2¼ lbs (1k) large potatoes
18 oz (500g) plain white flour
salt
ground black pepper
3 tomatoes, blanched, skinned,
pipped and diced

Serves 4

12 fresh sardines
2 fl oz (50ml) olive oil
1 fl oz (25ml) lemon juice
1 garlic clove, crushed
2 tablespoons parsley, chopped
ground black pepper
1 lemon (in quarters)
parsley to garnish

Boil unpeeled potatoes until soft but not coming apart. Remove from pan, peel and mash quickly. Blend in the flour, tomatoes and Parmesan until you have a smooth elastic mixture. Be careful not to over-knead or the result will be too heavy.

Roll the mixture into a sausage shape and cut into half inch discs. Press each disc with the prongs of a fork to shape with grooves, then lay them on a floured surface. Place in a large pan of boiling water and cook till they rise to the surface. Serve immediately, tossed in butter and sprinkled with grated Parmesan.

Mix the olive oil, lemon juice and garlic together and brush over sardines. Leave to marinate. Season and place·under hot grill for 3-4 minutes either side. Serve immediately with lemon wedges and sprinkle with chopped parsley.

BEDROOM FARCE

by **Alan Ayckbourn**

Lyttelton 16 March 1977 (West End from November 78)
Directors **Alan Ayckbourn & Peter Hall**
Ernest **Michael Gough**,
Delia **Joan Hickson**

DELIA, in her dressing gown, sits in front of her mirror and starts to remove her make-up. ERNEST enters with two plates

ERNEST Grub up.

DELIA Just a minute.

ERNEST It'll get cold.

DELIA I've just got to take this off.

ERNEST You can do that afterwards.

DELIA I'm not getting into bed with my make-up on, darling. It may look beautiful in the films but they don't have to worry about laundry bills.

ERNEST Oh well. Spot of bad news, anyway.

DELIA Bad news?

ERNEST Sardines were not in evidence. I had to settle for pilchards.

DELIA Pilchards? Oh . . .

ERNEST Don't you like pilchards?

DELIA Well, not as much.

ERNEST Similar. Both fish, anyway.

DELIA Yes.

ERNEST You had them in stock. I assumed you liked them.

DELIA I don't necessarily like everything I buy. Those were just stores. For an emergency.

ERNEST Ah, the old siege stores, eh?

DELIA I bought a little of everything. I think there's even some tinned red cabbage and I certainly don't intend to eat that.

ERNEST Oh well, I'll wolf the lot then, shall I?

DELIA No, no, leave me a little.

ERNEST Right. (He slides into bed) Aaah. Didn't put the blanket on, did we?

DELIA Nor we did.

ERNEST Ah. Woof. Down you go. (He shoves his feet into the bed) Ah, this is nice. What better way to end a day? Listening to the rain gushing through our roof . . .

DELIA It's not raining surely?

ERNEST Metaphorical. These aren't bad at all. You know, I think I could become a pilchard man in time.

SEAFOOD SAUSAGE

Serves 4

4 oz (125g) raw prawns, peeled
6 oz (150g) whiting fillet
6 oz (150g) salmon fillet
6 fl oz (175ml) double cream
1 large egg white
salt
ground white pepper
1 teaspoon chopped dill
half teaspoon chopped truffle
peelings
pinch nutmeg
dill sprigs to garnish

Reserve 2 oz (50g) of the prawns and chop roughly for texture. Purée the chilled whiting and remaining prawns and salmon in the processor. With the machine running add the egg white until well blended. Pass the purée through a fine sieve into a stainless steel bowl and refrigerate for 30 minutes.

Place stainless steel bowl over crushed ice and slowly beat in double cream with a wooden spoon. Season with salt, pepper and nutmeg, fold in the chopped prawns and truffle peelings. Butter four 10 x 10 inch (25cm) foil squares and divide mixture between them. Roll into sausage shapes and twist foil at both ends.

Poach the sausages at just under simmering point for 10-15 minutes or until firm to touch.

To serve, remove from foil, arrange on plate and surround with white wine and butter sauce (see page 30). Garnish with sprigs of dill.

MUSSELS IN GARLIC BUTTER

Serves 4

2 lbs (900g) live mussels
1 medium onion, chopped
6 fl oz (175ml) water
1 large garlic clove, crushed
2 oz (50g) finely chopped
shallots
3 tablespoons finely chopped
parsley
4 oz (125g) butter
salt
ground black pepper
parsley to garnish

Wash, scrub and de-beard mussels, discarding any that are open. Put the mussels in a large saucepan, scatter over the chopped onion, add the water and cover. Cook on a high heat shaking occasionally till mussels have opened-about 3 minutes. Allow to cool with lid removed.

Beat together the crushed garlic, chopped parsley, shallots and butter until smooth, season to taste. When mussels have cooled remove from pan with slotted spoon and discard the empty shell from each one.

Spread the garlic butter over the remaining mussels, divide onto oven-proof dishes and place in pre-heated oven gas mark 6 (400°f) (200°c) for about 10 minutes. Serve sprinkled with chopped parsley.

A FLEA IN HER EAR

by **Georges Feydeau**
translated by **John Mortimer**
Old Vic 8 February 1966,
Director **Jacques Charon**
Victor Emmanuel Chandebise **Albert Finney**, Tournel **John Stride**

CHANDEBISE Women have committed suicide for you ... True? Answer yes or no!

TOURNEL Just one actually.

CHANDEBISE Ah.

TOURNEL And besides, she recovered.

CHANDEBISE That's irrelevant!

TOURNEL Anyway the whole thing's a bit mysterious ... She poisoned herself eating mussels.

CHANDEBISE Mussels!

TOURNEL I'd just left her. She told everyone she did it in a fit of despair. But I must say I wouldn't choose a plate of moules marinières as a suicide weapon. Too risky.

NOISETTES OF PINK TROUT

Serves 4

4 oz (125g) salmon fillet
2 slices de-crusted white bread
2 oz (50g) butter
½ egg white
¾ oz (20g) onion, finely
chopped
2 tablespoons single cream
salt
ground white pepper
pinch ground nutmeg
4 fl oz (125ml) whipped
double cream
1 heaped teaspoon chopped
dill
8 x 3 oz (75g) skinned pink
trout fillets
3 fl oz (75ml) sour cream
lumpfish roe for garnish
sprigs of dill for garnish

Melt the butter and sweat the chopped onions without colouring. Allow to cool. Cut salmon into strips, place on stainless steel tray, cover with sliced bread, single cream and egg white. Season, cover and chill.

When cold, place in blender and purée. Place in stainless steel bowl and gradually beat in the whipped cream. Finally, stir in the chopped dill.

Flatten the trout fillets, season with salt and place on greased roasting foil, skin side uppermost, ensuring they overlap. Spread the purée over trout to cover completely. Roll over into cylindrical shape and tie at both ends. Poach in salted water for about 30 minutes. Remove and cool in refrigerator.

To serve, unwrap, slice and arrange on a plate. Serve with sour cream, garnished with lumpfish roe and sprigs of dill.

THE THREEPENNY OPERA
by **Bertolt Brecht**
Music **Kurt Weill**
English stage version by
Robert David MacDonald
Olivier 13 March 1986,
Director **Peter Wood**
Macheath **Tim Curry**,
Crookfingered Jake **Michael Bryant**

MACHEATH What's that in your hand, Jake?

JAKE A knife, Captain.

MACHEATH And what is that on your plate?

JAKE A trout, Captain.

MACHEATH I see. And with the knife, you are eating the trout, am I right? Jake, it is past comprehension, have you ever seen the like, Polly? eating his fish with a knife! Anyone who does that is no better than a pig, do I make myself plain, Jake?

Seafood Profiteroles with Fresh Herb and Fromage Frais Sauce

THE MAYOR OF ZALAMEA
by **Calderon De La Barca**
Translated by **Adrian Mitchell**
Cottesloe 12 August 1981, Olivier 7 December 1981,
Director **Michael Bogdanov**
Don Mendo **Daniel Thorndike,**
Nuno **Peter Løvstrøm**

DON MENDO But how could you
Know what is meet and what's not meet?

NUNO What's meat? A faintish memory...
Of what? Some fragrant, chewable,
Pink substance? No, I can't recall...
Such words as cheese – trout – pineapple,
Paella, brandy, turkey, ham
Sausage, sardines, sherry, shellfish –
Names of old friends I've not seen since
I thought meet to do you service.

DON MENDO When I say meet, I don't mean meat
But meet.

NUNO Let's see when you say meat,
You don't mean meat.

DON MENDO No

NUNO You mean meat.

DON MENDO Right.

NUNO It's true then, is it, sir?

DON MENDO True, what?

NUNO Hunger pains cause the brains to rot.

Serves 8

24 savoury choux buns
8 fl oz (225g) cream cheese
1 teaspoon grated horseradish
1 tablespoon single cream
salt
ground white pepper
6 oz (175g) smoked trout fillet
1 oz (25g) finely chopped onion
2 oz (50g) finely chopped roasted almonds

For the sauce

1 bunch fresh coriander
8 oz (225ml) fromage frais
2 tablespoons horseradish cream

Combine the cream cheese, single cream, horseradish, salt and pepper and mix till smooth. Flake the smoked trout fillets and add to the cream cheese mixture with the onion and almonds. Split the choux buns and fill with mixture.

Place picked coriander (reserving some for garnish), fromage frais and horseradish cream in processor and blend till smooth. Season to taste. To serve, arrange 3 buns on each plate, spoon sauce over and garnish with coriander sprigs.

SALMON TARTARE

Serves 4

12 oz (350g) fresh salmon fillet, skinned
salt
ground black pepper
juice of 1 lime
pinch cayenne pepper
1 small onion, finely chopped
1 teaspoon dill, chopped
1 oz (25g) chives, chopped
curly endive to garnish
8 slices brown toasted bread

Season the salmon fillets with salt, pepper, lime juice and cayenne pepper and then chop finely with sharp knife. Mix with the onion and dill and correct seasoning. Form small balls of the mixture and roll them in chopped chives.

To serve, arrange on plates on curly endive and accompany with toasted brown bread.

Marinated Salmon

THE DANCE OF DEATH
by **August Strindberg**
translated by **C D Locock**
Old Vic 21 February 1967,
Director **Glen Byam Shaw**
Captain **Laurence Olivier,**
Alice **Geraldine McEwan**

CAPTAIN What have you got for supper?

ALICE How should I know? Ask Kristin!

CAPTAIN Oughtn't mackerel to be in soon. It's autumn now!

ALICE Yes, it's autumn.

CAPTAIN Outside and in! But for all that, a broiled mackerel, with a slice of lemon, and a glass of white Burgundy, is not altogether to be despised.

ALICE You're getting quite eloquent.

Serves 4

1lb (450g) fresh salmon fillets, skinned

Pickling Ingredients

2 tablespoons granulated sugar
1½ tablespoons coarse sea salt
½ tablespoon ground black pepper
1½ tablespoons chopped dill
½ tablespoon sunflower oil

Mix the pickling ingredients in a bowl. Place salmon fillets skin-side down on chopping board, spread with the pickling ingredients. Wrap salmon and pickling ingredients in double foil, place in dish, put weight on top of fish and set in fridge for 48 hours or up to 5 days, turning every day.

Unwrap salmon, slice at an angle, slightly thicker than smoked salmon, arrange on plates and serve with a dill and mustard mayonnaise and rye bread and butter.

DILL AND MUSTARD SAUCE

1 pt (600 ml) mayonnaise
1 tablespoon Pommery or seed mustard
1 tablespoon chopped dill
lemon juice to taste
½ pt (150 ml) double cream

Mix together all the ingredients and season to taste.

Parma Ham and Fresh Figs

Serves 4

4 oz (125g) thinly sliced Parma ham
4 fresh figs
1 tablespoon olive oil
ground black pepper

Arrange the ham on plates. Cut a cross in the sharp end of figs, open like a flower, and place to one side of ham. Sprinkle with olive oil and ground black pepper. Serve with crusty French bread.

HERBY CHICKEN SAUSAGE

Serves 8

1 lb (450g) breast of chicken
meat, skinned and diced
2 egg whites
1 pint (570ml) double cream
1 teaspoon sage, chopped
1 teaspoon thyme, chopped
pinch nutmeg
salt
ground white pepper

Purée the chilled diced chicken in processor till smooth. With the processor still running, add the egg whites. Pass the purée through a fine sieve into a stainless steel bowl and chill for 30 minutes.

Place stainless steel bowl over crushed ice and slowly beat in the double cream with wooden spoon, season with salt, pepper and nutmeg and fold in the sage and thyme. Butter eight 10 x 10 inch (25cm) foil squares and divide mixture between them. Roll into sausage shapes and twist foil at both ends.

Poach the sausages at just under simmering point until firm to touch. Remove from pan and foil, place on tray, brush with butter and brown gently under the grill.

To serve, place sausage on plate and surround with watercress sauce. Garnish with a sprig of thyme and sage leaf.

WATERCRESS SAUCE

1 oz (25g) butter
2 shallots, finely chopped
2 bunches watercress, washed, stalks removed, and puréed
6 fl oz (175ml) double cream
4 fl oz (125ml) dry white wine
10 fl oz (275ml) chicken stock
salt
ground black pepper
8 sprigs thyme and
8 sage leaves for garnish

To make the sauce, melt the butter in a pan, add the shallots, cook until transparent, add the puréed watercress and cook for a further 2 minutes till watercress has softened. Add dry white wine and reduce until nearly evaporated. Add the chicken stock and reduce by half, pour in double cream and cook until coating consistency is achieved. Season to taste. Pass the sauce through a fine strainer and keep warm.

H, or Monologues at Front of Burning Cities
by **Charles Wood**
Old Vic 13 February 1969,
Director **Geoffrey Reeves**
Ensign Mullet **Benjamin Whitrow**

ENSIGN MULLET In the affair of the chupaties,

flat cakes of bread,

is popular in India,

was passed the one to the other

through the villages, I confess

the first chupatty I was

passed I had not any thought what

it was to signify,

to my sergeant,

what is this flat cake of bread,

and he replied it was a message of

some disturbing kind

and he took it off of me,

spread it with honey, had it to eat

and took sick,

would of died had he not recovered.

Duck Liver in Almond Mille-Feuille

Serves 8

1 lb duck liver foie gras
1 egg white
1 oz (25g) flour
2 oz (50g) butter, creamed
2 oz (50g) shredded almonds
pinch salt
grapes for garnishing

To make the almond pastry, lightly beat the egg white, then beat in the flour, creamed butter, almonds and salt. Roll to quarter-inch (0.5cm) thickness and spread on a well-buttered chilled baking tray (16 inch x 10 inch) (40cm x 25cm). Divide the pastry into four equal strips using a sharp knife.

Bake in pre-heated oven on gas mark 5 (375°f) (190°c), for 10-12 minutes. Cool, then divide the duck liver foie gras into three equal portions, ensuring it is soft enough to spread. Spread one third evenly on one strip of almond pastry and cover with another layer of pastry until all pastry is used. Press down lightly and smooth the sides with a palette knife. Chill for two hours.

To serve, slice across using a hot serrated knife, place on a plate and garnish with a few seedless white grapes.

MAIN COURSES

Tomato Tagliatelle
with Pesto Sauce

Serves 6

1 lb (450g) fresh tomato tagliatelle

For the PESTO SAUCE

36 leaves fresh basil, washed and dried carefully
large pinch rock salt
2 cloves garlic, crushed
2 oz (50g) pine kernels
2 tablespoons freshly grated Parmesan
3 fl oz (75ml) good quality olive oil
salt
ground black pepper
3 fl oz (75ml)double cream

Put the basil, salt and garlic into processor and reduce to a smooth green paste. Add the pine kernels and Parmesan cheese and blend in. Then add olive oil a little at a time with motor running until a smooth creamy texture is reached. Correct seasoning as required.

Put a few drops of oil into a large pan of salted boiling water. Toss in the fresh tagliatelle and cook for two minutes. Meanwhile place the double cream in a small pan, add the pesto mixture and heat gently. Drain the cooked pasta and add to sauce. Toss till fully coated and serve immediately with freshly grated Parmesan.

VEGETABLE RAGOÛT

Serves 4

4 oz (125g) of each of the
following prepared vegetables:
mange-tout
baby carrots
courgettes, sliced
button onions
button mushrooms
broccoli florets
cauliflower florets
haricots verts, cut 1 inch
(2.5cm) long

10 fl oz (275ml) vegetable
stock
1 tablespoon chives, chopped
½ tablespoon chopped tarragon
1 tablespoon chopped parsley
1 tablespoon cornflour
salt
pepper
1 oz (25g) butter
chervil to garnish

Bring vegetable stock to boil, blanch vegetables individually in the stock starting with the firmest. When all vegetables have been blanched and removed from stock, reduce by half.

Heat butter in another pan, add chopped herbs and sweat for a few minutes. Add herbs to stock pan, thicken with corn-flour to coating consistency. Return vegetables to stock, coat thoroughly.

Divide between four plates and garnish with chervil sprigs.

A MIDSUMMER NIGHT'S DREAM

by **William Shakespeare**
Cottesloe 25 November 1982, Lyttelton
12 April 1983 Director **Bill Bryden**
Titania **Susan Fleetwood,**
Bottom **Derek Newark**

TITANIA Or say, sweet love,
what thou desirest to eat.

BOTTOM Truly, a peck of
provender: I could munch your
good dry oats. Methinks I have
a great desire to a bottle of
hay: good hay, sweet hay, hath
no fellow.

TITANIA I have a venturous
fairy that shall seek

The squirrel's hoard, and fetch
thee thence new nuts.

BOTTOM I had rather have a
handful or two of dried pease.
But, I pray you, let none of
your people stir me: I have an
exposition of sleep come upon
me.

Spinach Roulade

Serves 4

1 lb (450g) fresh spinach
½ oz (10g) butter
salt
ground black pepper
ground nutmeg
4 eggs, separated
1 tablespoon grated Parmesan cheese

For the filling

½ oz (10g) butter
½ oz (10g) flour
8 oz (225g) button mushrooms, finely chopped
1 dessertspoon lemon juice
1 clove garlic, crushed
6 fl oz (175ml) milk
4 tablespoons double cream
salt
ground black pepper

To prepare the spinach mixture, remove any thick stalks and wash several times. Place in large saucepan and add 5 fl oz (150ml) of water, cover with lid and cook until tender. Remove lid halfway through cooking allowing liquid to reduce. When soft, drain, cool and squeeze out excess moisture. Blend in liquidizer with the butter, salt, pepper and nutmeg and put to one side.

Line a swiss roll tin with buttered greaseproof paper. Beat the 4 egg yolks into the spinach mixture. Adjust seasoning. Whip the 4 egg whites till stiff and fold into spinach mixture carefully, do not over-mix. Spread this mixture onto the tray and place into pre-heated oven, gas mark 5 (375°f) (190°c) for about 10 minutes. It should shrink from sides of tin. Remove from oven and keep warm.

To make the filling, melt butter in pan and add the crushed garlic. Cook without colouring. Add the chopped mushrooms and lemon juice, and cook till soft. Stir in the flour and gradually add milk, stirring continuously. Bring to the boil, reduce heat and allow to simmer for one minute. Add cream, adjust seasoning.

Place a large piece of greaseproof paper on worktop and sprinkle with parmesan. Turn the spinach cake upside down on to the Parmesan. Carefully peel off the greaseproof paper from spinach, spread the mushroom mixture over, and roll up like a Swiss roll. Slice through, arrange on plates and serve immediately.

THE MISANTHROPE

by **Molière**
English version by **Tony Harrison**
Old Vic 22 February 1973 (revived 9 July 1975), Director **John Dexter**
Célimène **Diana Rigg,**
Eliante **Jeanne Watts**
Lyttelton 26 May 1989, Director **Paul Unwin** (co-production with Bristol Old Vic),
Célimène **Sian Thomas,**
Eliante **Ingrid Craigie**

CELIMENE They only go to Cléon's for the food.

ELIANTE Cléon's cuisine though's not to be pooh-poohed.

CELIMENE The dinner turns to sawdust on one's lips

When Cléon's served with everything, like chips.

He tells a boring story, and you'd swear

The Château Mouton Rothschild's ordinaire.

Vegetable Filo Purse

Serves 4

4 sheets filo pastry, 12x8 inch (30x20cm)
1 lb (450g) cooked shredded spinach
4 oz (125g) ricotta cheese
2 oz (50g) toasted pine nuts
4 oz (125g) butter
salt
ground black pepper
nutmeg

Melt 1 oz (25g) of butter and add to cooked spinach in a bowl with the salt, pepper, nutmeg, pine nuts and ricotta cheese, combine evenly.

Lay out filo sheets, brush with the remaining butter and fold in half lengthways, brush again with butter. Divide the spinach mixture between the four sheets. Bring together the four corners of pastry and twist to form top of purse. Place on baking tray in pre-heated oven, gas mark 6 (400°f) (200°c) for 10 minutes until golden brown.

To serve, centre filo bag on each plate, surround with coulis and garnish with basil leaf. Serve immediately.

For the COULIS

12 oz (350g) ripe tomatoes
2 teaspoons vegetable oil
1 teaspoon lemon juice
1 small garlic clove, puréed
1 dessertspoon chopped basil
salt
ground white pepper

To make the coulis, blanch, skin, seed and chop the tomatoes. Place into processor and blend till smooth. Heat oil in pan, add garlic, cook without colouring. Add the basil and cook for a further minute, then add lemon juice and puréed tomatoes. Adjust seasoning. Reduce till smooth consistency.

VEGETARIAN STRUDEL

Serves 4

4 sheets filo pastry 12 x 8 inch
(30x20cm)
2 oz (50g) melted butter
4 slices goat's cheese ½ inch (1
cm) thick
2 tomatoes, blanched, seeded
and skinned
12 oz (350g) broccoli florets,
blanched
4 oz (125g) pesto paste (see
page 51)
ground black pepper
1 egg yolk
2 tablespoons sesame seeds

Lay filo pastry out and brush with butter, fold in half and brush again. Lay goat's cheese onto filo pastry, to one side.

Cut tomatoes into strips, lay on top of goat's cheese with broccoli and pesto paste. Adjust seasoning. Brush edges of pastry with butter and roll into parcel.

Place parcels onto greased baking sheet, brush with egg yolk, and sprinkle with sesame seeds. Bake in hot oven, gas mark 6 (400°f) (200°c) for 10-15 minutes.

WATCH ON THE RHINE
by **Lillian Hellman**
Lyttelton 16 September 1980,
Director **Mike Ockrent**
Babette Müller **Donna Angell,**
Fanny Farrelly **Peggy Ashcroft,**
Anise **Pauline Jameson,**
Bodo Müller **Timothy Breeze**

BABETTE (comes running in carrying a plate. She goes to FANNY) Eat it while it's hot, Grandma.

(FANNY peers down, takes the fork, begins to eat. ANISE and BODO both rise, move to FANNY, inspect the plate.)

FANNY (to them) Go away.

ANISE It is a potato pancake.

FANNY And the first good one I've eaten in many, many years. I love a good potato pancake.

BODO I likewise.

BABETTE I am making a great number for dinner.

SCAMPI PROVENÇALE

Serves 6

1½ lbs (700g) fresh peeled scampi
2 fl oz (60 ml) olive oil
4 oz (150g) shallots, finely diced
4 tomatoes, skinned, seeded and chopped
2 tablespoons white wine
2 oz (50g) stoned, chopped black olives
1 teaspoon tomato purée
2 cloves garlic, peeled and crushed
salt
pepper
1 tablespoon chopped parsley

Heat the olive oil in a pan, add the shallots and cook till soft. Then add the scampi, and cook for a further two minutes.

Add all the remaining ingredients except the parsley, cover the pan with lid and simmer for five minutes. Correct seasoning and consistency by reducing.

To serve, divide between plates, sprinkle over chopped parsley and serve with rice pilaff.

WINTER'S TALE
by **William Shakespeare**
Cottesloe 18 May 1988, Olivier 26 September 88, Director **Peter Hall**
Clown **Jeremy Flynn**

CLOWN Let me see; what am I to buy for our sheep-shearing feast? "Three pound of sugar; five pound of currants; rice" - what will this sister of mine do with rice? But my father hath made her mistress of the feast, and she lays it on. . . I must have saffron, to colour the warden pies; mace, dates, – none; that's out of my note: – nutmegs seven; a race or two of ginger, – but that I may beg; – four pound of prunes, and as many raisins o' the sun.

POACHED TROUT WITH FENNEL AND PERNOD SAUCE

Serves 4

4 x 8 oz (225g) cleaned fresh rainbow trout
4 oz (125g) finely sliced fennel
1½ oz (35g) butter
8 fl oz (225ml) dry white wine
4 fl oz (125ml) fish stock
2 oz (50g) shallots, finely chopped
salt
ground white pepper
¾ oz (15g) flour
¼ pint (150ml) double cream
2 fl oz (50ml) Pernod

In a buttered ovenproof dish, sprinkle the shallots and place trout on top. Add wine and fish stock, cover and bake for 10 minutes in oven, gas mark 7 (425°f) (220°c).

Remove from the oven and skin the trout carefully. Cover the fish with buttered greaseproof paper. Keep cooking liquor in a pan, and reduce by about a third.

Heat 1 oz (25g) butter in a separate pan, add the sliced fennel and slowly cook till soft. Add the flour and stir, pour in the Pernod and cook for a few seconds. Strain the reduced cooking liquor into this pot, bring to the boil. Add the cream and reduce to required consistency. Check seasoning.

Place trout on plates, cover with pernod sauce, garnish with sprigs of fennel ferns.

JOHN DORY FILLET WITH ASPARAGUS AND CHERVIL BUTTER SAUCE

Serves 4

8 fresh asparagus spears, peeled
16 button onions, peeled
1 bunch fresh chervil, chopped
4 x 4 oz (125g) John Dory
fillets
2 oz (50g) butter
2 oz (50g) finely chopped
shallots
squeeze of lemon juice
6 fl oz (175ml) dry white wine
5 fl oz (150ml) double cream
chervil sprigs for garnish

Slice the asparagus into one-and-a-half inch (3.5cm) lengths. Boil in plenty of salted water till just cooked, strain, refresh in ice water, drain and reserve. Poach the button onions till just tender in water.

Slice each John Dory fillet into 3 diagonal pieces. Butter an ovenproof dish, add the fish fillets and shallots and season with salt and pepper, then add the lemon juice and white wine. Cover and cook in moderate oven, gas mark 4 (350°f) (180°c) for 10 minutes. When cooked lift out fish, cover and keep warm.

Pour the cooking liquor into a saucepan and reduce by two thirds. Add the cream and reduce again till smooth. Whisk in the butter a little at a time, add the asparagus, button onions and chervil and check seasoning.

To serve, arrange the fish on 4 plates and pour over sauce. Garnish with sprigs of chervil.

LARK RISE
by **Keith Dewhurst** from **Flora Thompson's** book
Cottesloe 29 March 1978 (Revivals August 78, May 79, November 79), Directors **Bill Bryden** & **Sebastian Graham-Jones**
Laura **Caroline Embling**,
Jerry **Brian Glover**

(Gathered round Jerry Parish's barrow)

LAURA Oh. What's that?

JERRY That fish? That's a John Dory, my dear. See them black marks? Look like finger marks don't 'em? An' they do say that they be finger marks. He made 'em, that night, ye know, when they was fishin', ye know, and He took some and cooked 'em an' ever since they say that ivery John Dory as comes out of the sea have got His finger marks on 'em.

LAURA Do you mean the Sea of Galilee?

JERRY That's it, my dear. That's what they say; whether true or not of course I don't know, but there be the finger marks right enough, and that's what they say in our trade.

POACHED ESCALOPE OF SALMON WITH SORREL SAUCE

Serves 4

4 x 5 oz (150g) escalopes of
salmon fillet
4 fl oz (125ml) dry white wine
6 fl oz (175ml) fish stock
4 fl oz (125ml) double cream
2 oz (50g) finely chopped
shallots
2 tablespoons finely chopped
sorrel leaves
1 oz (25g) butter
salt
ground white pepper

Melt butter in an oven-proof dish, add shallots and place fish on top. Pour over the wine and stock and season. Cover and cook in moderate oven, gas mark 4 (350°f) (180°c) for approximately 5-10 minutes until firm to touch. Remove salmon from dish, cover and keep warm.

Strain the stock into a pan, reduce by half and add cream. Reduce again to a smooth consistency, add sorrel and correct seasoning.

To serve, arrange salmon on 4 plates and spoon over the sorrel sauce.

THE SHAUGHRAUN
by **Dion Boucicault**
Olivier 11 May 1988,
Director **Howard Davies**
Conn **Stephen Rea**,
Father Dolan **Robert Urquhart**

CONN I'm a vagabond entirely!

FATHER DOLAN What sort of life do you lead? What is your occupation? Stealing the salmon out of the river of a night!

CONN No, sir; I'm not so bad as that, but I'll confess to a couple o' throut – sure the salmon is out o'sayson.

(Pulls out two trout from his bag, and gives them to MOYA)

FR. DOLAN And don't you go poaching the grouse on the hillside?

CONN I do – divil a lie in it. (Pulls out two grouse)

FR. DOLAN D'ye know where all this leads to?

CONN Well, along wid the grouse, I'll go to pot.

SALMON PLAIT WITH GINGER SAUCE

Serves 4

4 x 6 oz (175g) middle fillets of fresh salmon
4 fl oz (125ml) dry white wine
6 fl oz (175ml) fish stock
4 fl oz (125ml) double cream
2 oz (50g) finely chopped shallots
½ oz (10g) freshly grated ginger
2 oz (50g) butter
salt
ground white pepper
1 tomato, blanched, skinned, seeded and chopped
4 sprigs dill

Lay salmon fillets on a board and make a cut down centre of each fillet lengthways, leaving one end intact. Overlap each side alternately until the plait is complete.

Melt butter in an ovenproof dish, add shallots and ginger and place salmon plaits on top. Add the white wine, fish stock and seasoning. Cover and cook in a moderate oven, gas mark 4 (350°f) (180°c) for approximately 5-10 minutes until firm to touch. Remove salmon, cover and keep warm.

Strain the stock into a pan and reduce by half. Add cream, reduce again until smooth consistency. Add the chopped tomato and correct seasoning.

To serve, flood the plate with the sauce and place the plait on top. Garnish with sprigs of dill.

Orange Glazed Brill Fillet

Serves 4

4 x 5 oz (150g) fillets of brill, skinned
1 oz (25g) butter
3 egg yolks
tablespoon of cold water
8 oz (225g) clarified butter
1 tablespoon of orange juice
zest of orange
4 fl oz (125ml) dry white wine
4 fl oz (125ml) fish stock
2 fl oz (50ml) double cream
1 oz (25g) finely chopped shallots
1 bunch watercress leaves, puréed
salt
ground white pepper

Melt butter in oven-proof dish, add the shallots and place in the fish fillets. Add the white wine and fishstock and season. Cover and cook in a moderate oven, gas mark 4 (350°f) (180°c) for approximately 5 minutes or until firm to touch.

When cooked, remove brill, cover and keep warm.

Strain stock into pan and reduce by half. Add the cream and reduce till smooth consistency. Add the puréed watercress, correct seasoning and keep warm.

To make orange glaze, combine the egg yolks and water in the top of a double boiler over hot water and whisk until they are light. Set the double boiler over a very low heat and whisk in the clarified butter a little at a time being careful not to overheat the sauce, or it will curdle. When all the butter has been whisked into yolks, the sauce should be thick and creamy. Season to taste with the salt, pepper and orange juice and keep warm.

To serve, place fish on a tray, spread with orange sauce and glaze under grill. Flood plates with watercress sauce (see page 48), and transfer fish to centre of plates.

Tagliatelle with Smoked Salmon and Dill

Serves 6

1½ lbs (700g) fresh tagliatelle verde
1 oz (25g) butter
ground black pepper
½ pint (275ml) double cream
1 tablespoon chopped dill
1 lb (450g) smoked salmon pieces
dill sprigs for garnish

In a large pan of boiling salted water, add one tablespoon of oil, then immerse and cook pasta until al dente. Drain, toss in the butter and keep warm.

Place double cream in separate pan, bring to the boil. Add smoked salmon pieces and dill, stir well and add to pasta pan with black pepper.

Serve immediately sprinkled with dill sprigs and freshly grated Parmesan.

Navarin of Monkfish

Serves 4

8 x 4 oz (125g) monkfish
steaks on bone
1 oz (25g) flour
2 tablespoons vegetable oil
4 oz (125g) button onions,
peeled and blanched
1 medium carrot, peeled and
diced
1 celery heart, diced
1 clove garlic, chopped
1 tomato, peeled, seeded and
diced
2 teaspoons tomato purée
1 teaspoon chopped dill
1 teaspoon chopped basil
4 fl oz (125ml) dry white wine
4 fl oz (125ml) fish stock
salt
ground black pepper
1 tablespoon chopped parsley

Toss the monkfish lightly in flour. Heat the oil in pan and sauté the fish till golden brown. Remove the fish from pan and reserve.

Place the carrot, garlic, button onions and celery into the pan and slowly cook to slightly soften. Return the fish to the pan, add the tomato, tomato purée, basil and dill and gently mix. Add the white wine and fish stock and bring gently to boil. Cover and place in oven, gas mark 4 (350°f) (180°c) for about 10 minutes. Remove from oven, lift out the fish and keep warm. Reduce the cooking liquor until required consistency. Correct seasoning.

To serve, place two fish steaks on each plate, spoon over the reduced sauce and garnish with chopped parsley. Serve with hot new potatoes.

JUMPERS
by **Tom Stoppard**
Old Vic 2 February 1972,
Director **Peter Wood**
Dotty **Diana Rigg**, George **Michael
Hordern**, Archie **Graham Crowden**
Lyttelton 21 September 1976,
Director **Peter Wood**
Dotty **Judith Paris**, George **Michael
Hordern**, Archie **Julian Glover**

DOTTY I must say, I do find
mashed potatoes and gravy
very consoling.

(GEORGE enters without
knocking)

GEORGE I'm sorry to interrupt
your inquiries –

(He looks round for the
Inspector. ARCHIE smoothly
takes a silver-backed notebook
from his pocket, and a silver
pencil from another)

ARCHIE When did you first
become aware of these feelings?

DOTTY (gaily) I don't know –
I've always found mashed
potatoes and gravy very consoling.

FISH RAGOÛT

Serves 6

2 fl oz (50ml) olive oil
1 large onion, finely chopped
2 large green peppers, cored,
seeded and chopped
2 lbs (900g) tomatoes, skinned,
seeded and chopped
2 large garlic cloves, finely
chopped
½ teaspoon fresh saffron
2 bay leaves
1 sprig of thyme
salt
ground black pepper
8 fl oz (350ml) dry white wine
10 fl oz (450ml) fish stock
1 tablespoon lemon juice
12 small clams, shells cleaned
12 mussels, shells cleaned
6 large prawns in shell
6 oz (175g) monkfish, cubed
8 oz (225g) small squid,
cleaned and cut into rings
1 teaspoon chopped dill
1 teaspoon chopped tarragon

In a casserole dish heat the oil and fry onion and peppers for 5 minutes. Add the tomatoes and cook until all liquid has evaporated.

Stir in the garlic, saffron, bay leaf, thyme, salt, pepper, wine, fish stock and lemon juice. Bring to the boil. Add the clams and mussels. Cover and reduce heat to medium. Cook for 10 minutes.

Add the prawns, monkfish and squid and cook for a further 5 minutes. Add dill and tarragon. Adjust seasoning and serve immediately in deep plates.

THE TEMPEST
by **William Shakespeare**
Old Vic 5 March 1974,
Director **Peter Hall**
Caliban **Denis Quilley**;
Cottesloe 19 August 1988, Olivier 29
September 1988, Director **Peter Hall**
Caliban **Tony Haygarth**

CALIBAN I prithee, let me bring thee where crabs grow;

And I with my long nails will dig thee pig-nuts;

Show thee a jay's nest and instruct thee how

To snare the nimble marmozet; I'll bring thee

To clust'ring filberts, and sometimes I'll get thee

Young scamels from the rock. Wilt thou go with me?

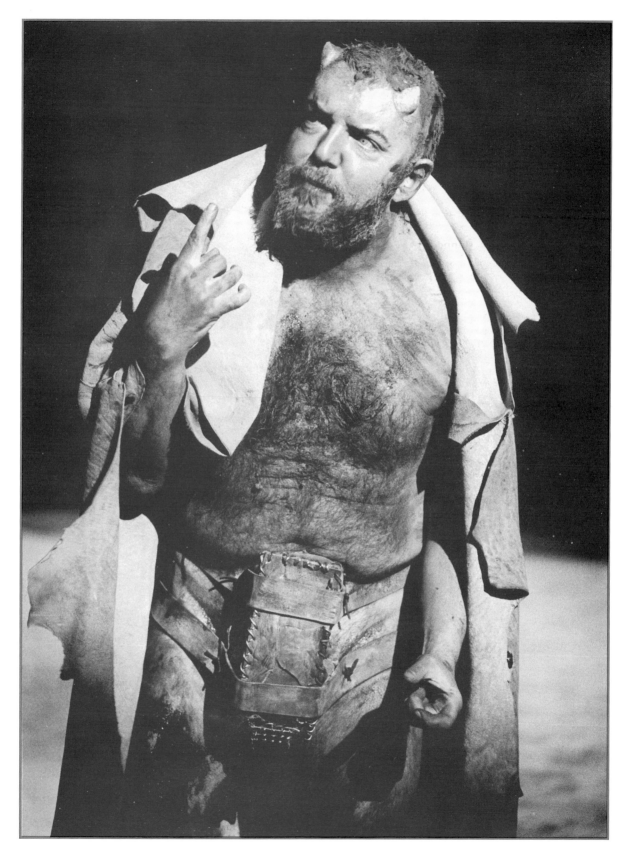

SALMON FISHCAKES WITH SORREL SAUCE

RACING DEMON
by **David Hare**
Cottesloe 8 February 1990,
Olivier 2 August 1990,
Director **Richard Eyre** °
Southwark **Richard Pasco,**
Lionel **Oliver Ford Davies**

The garden of Southwark's palace.

SOUTHWARK Lionel, it's always such a pleasure to see you.

LIONEL What a wonderful smell.

SOUTHWARK Indeed. My wife always fries her fishcakes in duckfat. It's not just the taste. It improves the texture as well.

LIONEL Goodness.

SOUTHWARK It's funny, yesterday you know we had the salmon. And there's no denying poached salmon's very nice. But all the time I was thinking, when do we get to the fishcakes?

LIONEL Ah yes.

(LIONEL stands a moment, waiting)

SOUTHWARK Same with lamb. A leg of lamb is also very nice. But isn't the whole point that next day you have shepherd's pie?

LIONEL Yes. Yes, well I know what you mean.

(LIONEL waits, confused. But SOUTHWARK seems oblivious)

SOUTHWARK And your wife? Heather? She cooks?

LIONEL Yes. Yes, frequently.

SOUTHWARK Good.

Serves 6

1 lb (450g) plain dry mashed potatoes
1 lb (450g) salmon fillet, skinned
1 tablespoon Dijon mustard
2 tablespoons Worcestershire sauce
salt and pepper to taste
2 teaspoons lemon juice
2 oz (50g) plain flour

For the sauce

3 oz (75g) shallots, finely chopped
1 bay leaf
few parsley stalks, chopped
½ tablespoon black peppercorns
8 fl oz (225ml) double cream
1 pint (570ml) water
5 fl oz (150ml) dry white wine
3 oz (75g) butter
3 oz (75g) flour
4 tablespoons sorrel, picked and shredded
dill sprigs for garnish

Apart from the butter, flour, cream and sorrel, simmer all the ingredients for the sauce for about 30 minutes or until reduced by half. When ready, pass this stock through fine sieve.

Place salmon on a deep tray and pour over the stock. Cover and place in moderate oven, gas mark 4 (350°f) (180°c) and cook until firm to touch – about 20 minutes. Remove salmon from stock and keep warm. Reserve stock.

In a pan melt the butter and slowly add the flour and stir over a low heat for about 5 minutes. Add the fish stock slowly whisking continuously and cook for about 10-15 minutes. Pass through a fine sieve, return to pan, add double cream, sorrel, salt and pepper to taste. Cook until coating consistency is achieved. Keep hot for serving.

For the fishcakes, mix the mashed potatoes, salmon, mustard, lemon juice and Worcestershire sauce in a mixing bowl, making sure the salmon is broken into small flakes. Mould the mixture into 6 cakes, roll them in the remaining flour to coat and prevent sticking. Shallow pan fry until brown, then transfer to oven to bake for a further 10–15 minutes, gas mark 8 (450°f) (230°c) until hot in the middle.

To serve, flood the plates with sorrel sauce, place the fishcake on top and garnish with dill sprigs.

Seafood Wellington

Serves 6

1 lb (450g) salmon fillet, skinned
1 lb (450g) brill fillet
14 oz (400g) puff pastry
1 egg, beaten
4 oz (125g) button mushrooms, wiped and chopped
2 oz (50g) shallots, finely chopped
1 oz (25g) butter
1 tablespoon chopped dill
salt
ground black pepper
1 teaspoon lemon juice
2 fl oz (50ml) dry white wine

Melt the butter in a pan, place in the chopped shallots and mushrooms and cook until softened. Add the lemon juice and white wine and cook until nearly evaporated. Add the double cream, season to taste and cook until thick consistency is obtained. Allow to cool and reserve.

Roll out the pastry into a rectangle 14 x 12 inch (35 x 30cm). Place the salmon fillet in centre of pastry, skinned side up. Spread with mushroom mix and sprinkle with chopped dill. Top with the brill fillet. Trim pastry to 4 inch (10cm) border reserving trimmed pastry for garnish. Brush edges of pastry with beaten egg. Fold pastry over the fish and wrap up like a parcel. Place on baking sheet, sealed edges down, brush with beaten egg. Roll out pastry trimmings and cut into fish shapes. Place on top of parcel to decorate. Bake in oven, gas mark 7 (425°f)(220°c) for about 25 minutes until pastry is golden brown.

To serve, cut into six slices and garnish with parsley sprigs.

SALMON TROUT IN FILO PASTRY

Serves 4

4 x 5 oz (150g) salmon trout fillet, skinned
4 sheets filo pastry, 12 x 8 inch (30 x 20cm)
4 oz (125g) fennel, cooked and shredded
5 oz (150g) butter
1 tablespoon lemon juice
salt
ground black pepper
chopped fennel ferns
1 teaspoon sesame seeds

Lay out filo sheets and brush with butter. Fold sheets in half lengthways, brush again with butter.

Place the cooked fennel, lemon juice, a little melted butter and chopped fennel ferns onto the pastry sheets. Place the salmon fillets on top, skinned side up. Fold up like a parcel, brush with melted butter and sprinkle with sesame seeds. Place on baking sheet and cook in pre-heated oven, gas mark 6 (400°f) (200°c) until golden brown.

Serve immediately with white wine and butter sauce (see page 30). Garnish with dill.

SEAFOOD PIE

Serves 8

1 lb (450g) sole fillet cut in
strips
1 lb (450g) salmon fillet cut in
strips
6 oz (175g) peeled raw prawns
6 oz (175g) scallops, diced
6 oz (175g) mushrooms, wiped
and sliced
1 lb (450g) puff pastry
1 egg, beaten
2 oz (50g) shallots, chopped
3 oz (75g) butter
2 oz (50g) flour
5 fl oz (150ml) fish stock
5 fl oz (150ml) dry white wine
5 fl oz (150ml) double cream
1 tablespoon chopped dill
salt
pepper

Melt 1 oz (25g) butter in a pan. Add the shallots and cook till softened. Add the white wine and reduce by half. Add the fish stock and reduce by half again. Then add the cream.

In another pan, melt 2 oz (50g) butter, stir in the flour and cook for 5 minutes without colouring. Slowly add the reduced liquor to the roux, stirring until smooth consistency is achieved. Pass through a fine sieve, then add chopped dill. Reserve and leave to cool.

Layer individual china scallop dishes with the sole, salmon, prawns, scallops and mushrooms and cover with the cooled sauce. Roll out the pastry, cut into 8 tops and place over egg washed scallop dishes. Trim the edges and use trimmings for decoration. Brush with beaten egg and make small incision on top. Bake in oven gas mark 6 (400°f) (200°c) for about 15-20 minutes or until pastry is golden brown. Serve immediately.

THE BROWNING VERSION
by **Terence Rattigan**
Lyttelton 13 May 1980,
Director **Michael Rudman**
Millie Crocker-Harris **Geraldine McEwan**, Mrs Gilbert **Mary Chilton**, Gilbert **Peter Bourke**

MILLIE The headmaster's just coming up the drive. Don't tell him I'm in. The fish pie isn't in the oven yet.

MILLIE And the kitchen is in a terrible mess. I'm in the middle of cooking dinner –

MRS GILBERT Oh. Do you cook?

MILLIE Oh, yes. I have to. We haven't had a maid for five years.

MRS GILBERT Oh, I do think that's wonderful of you. I'm scared stiff of having to do it for Peter – I know the first dinner I have to cook for him will wreck our married life –

GILBERT Highly probable.

MILLIE Well, these days we've all got to try and do things we weren't really brought up to do.

COULIBIAC

Serves 8

1¾ lbs (750g) skinned salmon
fillet
3 tablespoons chopped dill
4 oz (125g) butter
8 oz (225g) diced onion
5 oz (150g) long grain rice
8 fl oz (225ml) fish stock
7 oz (200g) chopped cooked
mushrooms
2 hard boiled eggs, chopped
¼ pint (150ml) fish velouté
(see page 21)
1 tablespoon chopped parsley
1 lb (450g) puff pastry
2 oz (50g) flour
1 egg yolk
salt
pepper

Cut the salmon into ¾
inch (1.5cm) slices.
Sprinkle with salt, pep-
per and 1 tablespoon of
chopped dill. Chill and leave
to marinate for at least 2 hours
or overnight.

Heat 1 oz (25g) of butter in a
pan, add 2 oz (50g) of diced
onion and cook till softened.
Add rice and stir. Add the fish
stock with a little salt. Cover
and transfer to pre-heated
moderate oven, gas mark 4
(350°f) (180°c) for about 18
minutes until rice is tender and
all liquid is absorbed. Remove
from oven and leave to cool.

Heat another 1 oz (25g) of
butter and cook the rest of the
diced onion. Leave to cool.
Mix the cool rice with diced
onion, mushrooms, eggs, fish
velouté, parsley, remaining dill
and butter. Adjust seasoning.

Roll out half the pastry into a
rectangle about ⅛ of an inch
(0.25cm) thick. Cover with a
quarter of the rice mixture
leaving a ¾ inch (1.5cm) rim.
Continue with layers of marinated salmon and rice mixture
till all mixture is used. Roll out
the remaining pastry into a
slightly larger rectangle. Brush
the base rim with beaten egg,
cover with pastry and press the
edges firmly together, neatly.
Make a small hole on top and
insert pastry funnel. Decorate
with pastry trimmings. Brush
with beaten egg. Place on baking sheet and bake for about
40-45 minutes at gas mark 7
(425°f) (220°c) until golden
brown. Slice and serve immediately.

SALSICCE E FAGIOLE
(ITALIAN SAUSAGE WITH BEANS)

Serves 4

8 Italian sausages (preferably pork)
1 pint cannellini beans (soaked for 48 hours in cold water)
½ teaspoon salt
6 cloves garlic, peeled
4 tablespoons olive oil
4 fresh sage leaves
1 tablespoon tomato purée

Drain the beans and boil in about 4 pints (2.25 lts) of water for about 1½ - 2 hours till soft.

Then add the salt and 4 of the garlic cloves. Cook for a further 20 minutes. Then add the sausages and cook for 15 minutes.

Heat the oil in a large frying pan. Crush the remaining 2 cloves of garlic and fry for about 5 minutes without colouring. Remove the sausages from the beans, add to frying pan, and brown all over.

Add the beans, sage and tomato purée, cover and simmer for 15 minutes. Serve immediately.

CALVES' LIVER AND RED ONIONS

Serves 4

8 x 2½ oz (65g) thin slices of calves' liver
1 lb (450g) thinly sliced red onions
2½ fl oz (65ml) olive oil
1 oz (25g) butter
1 teaspoon fresh thyme leaves, chopped
1 tablespoon lemon juice
salt
ground black pepper
chopped parsley

Place half the oil and butter in frying pan with the red onions and thyme. Cover the pan and cook on very low heat for 1 hour, until shiny and soft. After 1 hour, add the lemon juice and seasoning.

In another pan place the remaining oil and butter and heat. Season the liver slices and quickly fry until golden brown both sides, keeping slightly pink in the middle.

To serve, arrange the red onions on four plates and divide the liver between four plates. Garnish with chopped parsley.

BRIGHTON BEACH MEMOIRS
by **Neil Simon**
Lyttelton 25 February 1986 (West End
from November 1986),
Director **Michael Rudman**
Jack **Harry Towb**, Eugene **Stephen
Mackintosh**, Kate **Frances de la Tour**

JACK Somebody has some-
thing to discuss? If there's a
problem, this is the time to
bring it up. This is the family
hour.

EUGENE What a great idea
for a radio show. The Family
Hour. Every Wednesday night
you hear a different family eating dinner discussing their
problems of the week. And you
get to hear different recipes.
(As announcer) "WEAF pre-
sents dinner at Brighton Beach
starring the Jacob Jerome
Family and featuring tonight's

specialty, liver and cabbage,
brought to you by Ex-Lax, the
mild laxative."

KATE The whole country's
going to hear about a fifteen-
year-old boy gagging on liver?

Sautéed Duck Livers en Brioche

CAT ON A HOT TIN ROOF

by **Tennessee Williams**
Lyttelton 3 February 1988,
Director **Howard Davies**
Maggie **Lindsay Duncan**

MARGARET (shouting above the roar of water) One of those no-neck monsters hit me with a hot buttered biscuit so I have t'change!

Serves 4

1 lb (450g) duck livers, trimmed of sinew
4 oz (125g) wild mushrooms
2 oz (50g) chopped shallots
5 fl oz (150ml) chicken stock
3 fl oz (75ml) madeira
2 fl oz (50ml) red wine
1 oz (25g) butter
1 teaspoon thyme, chopped
1 fresh baked brioche loaf
1 tablespoon oil
4 sprigs thyme for garnish

To make sauce, sweat the shallots in the butter with chopped thyme, madeira and red wine and reduce by half. Then add the chicken stock and reduce to coating consistency. Correct seasoning, keep warm.

Place the oil in frying pan and over high heat, fry the duck livers until browned but pink in centre. Remove from pan and keep warm. Reduce heat, add the mushrooms to the frying pan, add madeira sauce and cook for a few seconds. Return duck livers to pan.

To serve, place one slice of warmed brioche on each plate and top with contents of pan. Garnish with sprigs of thyme.

CHICKEN SUPRÊME WITH RED PEPPER MOUSSELINE

Serves 8

8 x 7 oz (200g) chicken breasts
4 oz (125g) chicken breast
meat finely diced
1 small egg white
5 fl oz (150ml) double cream
1 oz (25g) red peppers,
skinned and puréed
salt
pepper
chicken stock to poach

Purée the diced chicken breast meat in processor until smooth. With the processor still running, add the egg white. Pass through a fine sieve into stainless steel bowl. Place bowl over crushed ice and slowly beat in double cream with a wooden spoon. Season with salt and pepper and fold in the red pepper purée.

Make incision in chicken breasts and pipe in equal amounts of mousseline mixture. Seal with cocktail sticks. To cook, poach in chicken stock at simmering point for about 10-15 minutes or until the breast is firm.

To serve, slice through chicken breast to expose mousseline and put onto plates. Serve with watercress sauce (see page 48).

MOTHER COURAGE
by **Bertolt Brecht**
translated by **Eric Bentley**
Old Vic 12 May 1965.
Director **William Gaskill**
Cook **Frank Finlay**,
Chaplain **Peter Cellier**

COOK Chaplain, peace makes me sick. Mankind must perish by fire and sword, we're born and bred in sin! Oh, how I wish I was roasting a great fat capon for the Commander – God knows where he's got to – with mustard sauce and those little yellow carrots

CHAPLAIN Red cabbage – with capon, red cabbage.

COOK You're right. But he always wanted yellow carrots.

CHAPLAIN He never understood a thing.

CHICKEN WITH GIN AND DILL SAUCE

Serves 6

6 x 7 oz (200g) chicken breasts
1 oz (25g) butter
2 oz (50g) shallots, finely diced
5 fl oz (150ml) chicken stock
4 fl oz (125ml) double cream
zest of 1 lemon
juice of 1 lemon
2 fl oz (50ml) gin
1 tablespoon chopped dill
dill sprigs for garnish

Melt butter in a pan and cook chicken until golden brown on both sides, approximately 10 minutes. Remove from pan and keep warm.

Add shallots to the pan and cook till softened. Deglaze with the gin and juice of one lemon. Reduce by half, add chicken stock and reduce again by half till syrupy consistency is achieved. Pass through fine sieve, return to pan and add cream and chopped dill and zest of lemon.

To serve, place chicken on plates and surround with sauce. Garnish with dill sprigs.

CHICKEN BREASTS FILLED WITH CREAM CHEESE, GARLIC AND CHIVES

Serves 4

4 x 7 oz (200g) chicken breasts
4 oz (125g) cream cheese
1 bunch chopped chives
1 clove garlic, crushed
salt
ground black pepper
1 oz (25g) butter
1 fl oz (25ml) vegetable oil

Place cream cheese, two-thirds of the chives, garlic, salt and pepper in a bowl and combine thoroughly. Make incision in chicken breast and fill with cheese mixture, secure breasts with cocktail sticks.

Heat oil and butter in pan and sauté until golden brown on both sides.

Remove cocktail sticks and place on plates, garnish with remaining chopped chives and surround with tomato coulis (see page 55).

BREAST OF DUCK WITH BLACKCURRANTS AND CASSIS

Serves 8

4 x 10 oz (275g) duck magrets
(breasts), trimmed
1 clove garlic, chopped
1 oz (25g) shallots, finely
chopped
4 oz (125g) chilled butter
4 oz (125g) blackcurrants
8 fl oz (225ml) poultry stock
4 fl oz (125ml) red wine
1 thyme sprig
2 tablespoons blackcurrant jam
2 fl oz (50ml) crème de cassis
8 bay leaves
2 fl oz (50ml) vegetable oil

Score the fat on the duck breasts. Heat oil in thick bottomed pan and add the duck breasts bone-side down. Cook until brown, turn onto skin-side and seal to prevent juices escaping. Place into hot oven, gas mark 7 (425°f) (220°c) for about 5-10 minutes ensuring the breasts are very pink when removed. Set aside, keep warm to rest.

Discard excess fat from pan. Add 1 oz (25g) of butter to pan, add shallots, garlic and half of the blackcurrants and cook until soft. Add the red wine and jam and reduce by half. Add the poultry stock and thyme and reduce again to coating consistency. Correct seasoning. Pass through sieve into a clean pan. Add the crème de cassis, bring to a simmer and slowly add the chilled butter piece by piece to give shiny appearance.

To serve, slice the rested duck breasts at an angle and arrange on plates. Surround with cassis sauce, sprinkle with blackcurrants and garnish with bay leaf.

THE MISER

by **Molière**
translated by **Jeremy Sams**
Olivier 9 May 1991,
Director **Steven Pimlott**
Harpagon **Charles Kay,**
Maître Jacques **David Ross,**
Valère **Adrian Rawlins**

HARPAGON Maître Jacques – this evening I've invited people to supper.

M. JACQUES Well that's a first.

HARPAGON So tell me, can you give us a decent meal?

M. JACQUES If you give me some decent money.

HARPAGON Money, always money. All they ever talk about is money, money, money. The only word on their lips – money. That's all they say to me. Money. Money. Money – they're obsessed.

VALERE I've never heard such impertinence in all my life. Having to spend a lot of money on a good meal, indeed! Any fool could do that. No, the trick, the real skill is getting a good meal for very little money.

M. JACQUES A good meal for very little money?

VALERE Ah yes.

M. JACQUES Well you'll have to let us in on that particular secret. Why don't you take my job as cook? You seem to be the boss around here.

HARPAGON Shut up. Tell me, how can it be done?

M. JACQUES Ask him. It's his idea.

HARPAGON No, I want you to tell me.

M. JACQUES Fine. How many guests are there?

HARPAGON We'll be eight or ten – but only cater for eight – if eight people have got enough, that's enough for ten.

VALERE Very true.

M. JACQUES Right. So we'll start with four different soups, five main dishes – let's see – soups, entrées, side salads...

HARPAGON Stop! Do you want me to feed the whole town?

M. JACQUES Then there's the joints – beef, pork, mutton ...

HARPAGON Stop – you're eating up all my resources.

M. JACQUES Then puddings of course.

HARPAGON Oh, this is too much.

VALERE It is ... Do you want to stuff them till they burst? Do you want Monsieur to murder his guests? Haven't you read about the ill effects of overeating? Don't you know that a surfeit can endanger people's health?

HARPAGON He's absolutely right.

VALERE Maître Jacques, you obviously don't know that a full table is a potential threat to life and limb. And that true hospitality is in frugality – excess is an unpardonable insult. And that you must follow this dictum "Eat to live, but do not live to eat".

HARPAGON Oh, beautifully put. I love your dictum. I embrace you for it. It's the best dictum I've ever heard. What was it again? Live to eat, not eat ... no, that's not right. How did it go?

VALERE "Eat to live, not live to eat."

HARPAGON And which great philosopher said that?

VALERE The name escapes me for the moment.

HARPAGON Write it out for me – I'll have it engraved in letters of gold – it'll look nice above the mantelpiece in the dining room.

VALERE It will be done. As for supper, leave it to me. I'll organise everything.

HARPAGON It's in your hands

M. JACQUES Good. That'll keep mine clean.

HARPAGON Now, we'll need something nice and filling – so they don't need to overeat. Beans, say, lots of fat, pie well stuffed with chestnuts and suet dumplings.

VALERE Sounds delicious. Rely on me.

TRADITIONAL ROAST GOOSE

Serves 10

1 x 10 1b (4.5k) fresh goose (oven ready)
1 oz (25g) butter
½ bunch sage
1 medium peeled onion
salt
pepper

Place the sage and onion inside the prepared bird with a little seasoning. Rub the butter over the goose and season with salt and pepper. Place one cup of water into wire racked roasting tray and place goose on top. Cook in moderately hot oven, gas mark 7 (425°f) (220°c) allowing 15 minutes per lb (450g) plus 15 minutes extra.

Prick the skin surface every 30 minutes to release excess fat. When cooked, remove from oven and keep warm. Tip off fat from tray and make a thickened gravy with this stock.

Serve the goose with thickened gravy, apple sauce and sage and onion stuffing.

AT OUR TABLE
by **Daniel Mornin**
Cottesloe 17 September 1991,
Director **Jenny Killick**
Richard **Nicholas Woodeson**,
Anna **Cathryn Harrison**

RICHARD You got the goose?

(ANNA looks up)

ANNA ·Goose?

RICHARD Goose.(Slight pause)

ANNA I bought some sausages.

RICHARD Sausages?

(Slight pause)

ANNA Where would I find a goose?

RICHARD You're teasing.

ANNA Is he too grand for sausages?

RICHARD Oh really.

ANNA Perhaps you'd better take him off to a restaurant.

RICHARD He asked to eat here.

ANNA To remind him of how ordinary folk live.

(There is a silence)

RICHARD I imagine he wants a quiet evening.

ANNA Then he'll have a quiet family meal. (Pause) I'm sure he's sick to death of rich food. . (She looks up from her sewing) Is he fat?

RICHARD Fat?

ANNA Power makes men fat.

RICHARD Is that so.

(Silence)

ANNA It is so.

(Richard sighs)

RICHARD I repeatedly told you to buy a goose.

(Silence. Anna returns to her sewing.)

ANNA Where?

RICHARD Anywhere! We're surrounded by farms.

(Pause)

ANNA I saw one paddling in a pond.

RICHARD Did you.

(Slight pause)

ANNA Perhaps I should've jumped in after it with a knife?

RICHARD You really are very childish.

ANNA Sausages.

RICHARD I know you're trying to annoy me.

ANNA Sausages.

RICHARD Stop it.

ANNA Sausages.

(Cold silence)

Of course I got your stupid goose.

ROAST LEG OF LAMB WITH SHREWSBURY SAUCE

Serves 6–8

4 lb (1.8k) fresh English leg of lamb
2 tablespoons vegetable oil
salt
ground black pepper
2 sprigs rosemary
1 tablespoon red wine vinegar

For the sauce

4 oz (125g) fresh redcurrants
2 oz (50g) redcurrant jelly
4 fl oz (125ml) port wine
1 teaspoon prepared English mustard
salt
ground black pepper
rosemary for garnish

The meat should be at room temperature. Place in roasting tin, spread with the oil, rosemary and seasoning. Roast at gas mark 6 (400°f) (200°c) for 1–1 ½ hours basting frequently. Remove from oven and rest for 10 minutes.

While the lamb is resting, tip off excess fat from baking tray and reheat the tray on a ring to solidify the residual liquor. Add the port wine, and vinegar and reduce by half. Add ½ pint (275ml) water, redcurrant jelly, English mustard and seasoning and stir. Reduce again by a half. Thicken to desired consistency and pass through fine sieve into another pan. Add the fresh redcurrants and keep warm.

To serve, spoon sauce to side of sliced lamb and garnish with rosemary.

NAPOLI MILIONARIA

by **Eduardo de Filippo**
English version by **Peter Tinniswood**
Lyttelton 27 June 1991,
Director **Richard Eyre**
Errico **Mark Strong**,
Gennaro **Ian McKellen**

ERRICO Don Gennaro, this is the little birthday supper I was telling you about. Roast lamb, roast potatoes and all the trimmings.

GENNARO Roast lamb! Ye Gods, that looks good. And it smells delicious. You know, there were times when if something like that had come our way, we'd have killed for it. Ripped each other apart with our bare hands. God, what times those were.

LOIN OF LAMB WITH ROSEMARY

Serves 6–8

3 lb (1.4k) loin of lamb (chined)
2 large garlic cloves, slivered
½ tablespoon fresh rosemary
1 teaspoon fresh chopped oregano
juice of 1 lemon
2 oz (50g) soft butter
salt
ground black pepper

Cut small slits into the surface of the loin with sharp pointed knife. Insert the slivers of garlic. Combine the rosemary and oregano with the lemon juice, softened butter, and freshly ground black pepper. Spread the mixture over fleshy side of loin of lamb. Leave the lamb to stand at room temperature until it has lost its chill.

Stand the lamb on a rack in a roasting tin, place in oven, gas mark 4 (350°f) (180°c) for about one hour (20 minutes per lb), basting occasionally.

When cooked, transfer lamb to heated platter and rest in a warm place for 10 minutes before carving. Make gravy with residue in roasting pan by tipping off excess fat, adding ½ pint water and reducing to desired consistency.

THE BEAUX' STRATAGEM

by **George Farquhar**

Old Vic 8 April 1970, Director **William Gaskill**, Mrs Sullen **Maggie Smith**, Country Woman **Mary Griffiths**
Lyttelton 14 November 1989, Director **Peter Wood**, Mrs Sullen **Brenda Blethyn**, Country Woman **Rita Davies**

MRS SULLEN Were I born an humble Turk, where women have no soul nor property, there I must sit contented. But in England, a country whose women are its glory, must women be abused? where women rule, must women be enslaved? Nay, cheated into slavery, mocked by a promise of comfortable society into a wilderness of solitude! I dare not keep the thought about me. O, here comes something to divert me.

(Enter a COUNTRY WOMAN)

COUNTRY WOMAN I come, an't please your ladyship – you're my Lady Bountiful, an't ye?

MRS SULLEN Well, good woman, go on.

COUNTRY WOMAN I come seventeen long mail to have a cure for my husband's sore leg.

MRS SULLEN Your husband! What, woman, cure your husband!

COUNTRY WOMAN Ay, poor man, for his sore leg won't let him stir from home.

MRS SULLEN There, I confess, you have given me a reason. Well, good woman I'll tell you what you must do. You must lay your husband's leg upon a table, and with a chopping knife you must lay it open as broad as you can; then you must take out the bone, and beat the flesh soundly with a rolling pin; then take salt, pepper, cloves, mace, and ginger, some sweet herbs, and season it very well; then roll it up like brawn, and put it into the oven for two hours.

COUNTRY WOMAN Heavens reward your ladyship! I have two little babies too that are piteous bad with the graips, an't please ye.

MRS SULLEN Put a little pepper and salt in their bellies, good woman.

BOILED LEG OF MUTTON WITH CAPER SAUCE

Serves 10–12

9-lb (4k) leg of mutton
(trimmed)
salt
2 onions, stuck with cloves
4 large carrots, peeled
1 large bouquet garni (parsley,
thyme, winter savory)

For the caper sauce

2 oz (50g) butter
10 fl oz (275ml) cooking liquid
from mutton
2 oz (50g) flour
4 tablespoons capers (plus a
little of the juice)
1 tablespoon white wine
vinegar
ground black pepper

Place the mutton into a deep pan and cover with water. Bring to the boil, skim thoroughly then add one tablespoon of salt and simmer for 20 minutes. Add a cup of cold water and shake pan to bring up the scum. Skim again until liquor is clear. Adjust the heat so that water is simmering gently. Add the vegetables and bouqet garni and cook for about 2½ hours. When cooked, leave to one side in pot until needed.

In another pan make a roux with butter and flour, chop one tablespoon of capers and add to roux with the juice of capers and wine vinegar. Slowly add the 10 fl oz (275ml) of mutton stock, stirring all the while, until the consistency of double cream. Pass through a fine sieve into a clean pan. Add the remaining capers. Adjust seasoning.

To serve, remove mutton from pan, carve and serve immediately with the caper sauce and sprinkle with chopped parsley.

THREE SISTERS
by **Anton Chekhov**
translated by **Moura Budberg**
Old Vic 4 July 1967,
Director **Laurence Olivier**
Chebutikin **Paul Curran**,
Solionij **Frank Wylie**

CHEBUTIKIN And the meal was in true Caucasian style too: onion soup and Chekartma, as the meat dish.

SOLIONIJ Cheremsha isn't meat, it's a vegetable like our onion.

CHEBUTIKIN No, my angel. Chekartma is not an onion, it's mutton.

SOLIONIJ And I tell you that Cheremsha is onion.

CHEBUTIKIN And I tell you that Chekartma is mutton.

SOLIONIJ And I tell you that Cheremsha is onion.

CHEBUTIKIN Why do I argue with you? You've never been to the Caucasus, nor eaten Chekartma.

SOLIONIJ I haven't eaten it because I dislike it, it stinks, that Cheremsha, just like onion.

PORK TENDERLOIN WITH PLUM SAUCE

SHE STOOPS TO CONQUER
by **Oliver Goldsmith**
Lyttelton 8 November 1984,
Director **Giles Block**
Marlow **Hywel Bennett,**
Hastings **Gregory Floy,**
Hardcastle **Tom Baker**

MARLOW (Reading) For the first course at the top, a pig's face, and prune sauce.

HASTINGS Damn your pig's face, I say.

MARLOW And damn your prune sauce, say I.

HARDCASTLE And yet, gentlemen, to men that are hungry, a pig's face, with prune sauce, is very good eating.

MARLOW At the bottom, a calf's tongue and brains.

HASTINGS Let your brains be knocked out, my good sir; I don't like them.

MARLOW Or you may clap them on a plate by themselves. I do.

Serves 4

2 tablespoons olive oil
4 x 5 oz (150g) pork fillets, trimmed
4 fl oz (125ml) dry sherry
10 fl oz (275ml) chicken stock
2 tablespoons hoisin sauce
1 tablespoon tomato purée
1 tablespoon plum jam
½ lb (225g) fresh red plums, peeled and halved
ground black pepper
salt
chopped parsley for garnish

Heat the oil in a flameproof dish and brown pork fillets on both sides. Reduce the heat and add the sherry, stock, hoisin sauce, tomato purée and plum jam to the pan. Bring to the boil. Reduce heat again and simmer for 8-10 minutes. Then add the plums. Lift out the pork fillets and keep hot to one side.

Cook the sauce until reduced by half. Season. To serve, slice pork fillets into medallions, arrange on plates and spoon over plums and sauce. Garnish with chopped parsley.

Pork Loin with Gin and Juniper Berries

Serves 6

4 lb (1.8k) pork loin (boned
and skinned)
2 cloves garlic, slivered
20 juniper berries, toasted and
lightly crushed
salt
ground black pepper
5 fl oz (150ml) veal stock
5 fl oz (150ml) dry white wine
2 fl oz (50ml) gin
2 sage leaves, chopped
2 oz (50g) shallots, finely
chopped

With a sharp pointed knife make slits on the inside of loin and insert slivers of garlic and half the juniper berries. Roll up and tie tightly with string. Season with salt and pepper.

Stand on a wire racked roasting tin and cook in a moderate oven, gas mark 5 (375°f) (190°c) for 2 hours, basting occasionally or until the juices run clear. Transfer pork to heated dish and keep warm.

Tip off excess fat from dish, place in shallots and cook on ring till softened. Add chopped sage, remaining juniper berries and the gin. Cook until nearly evaporated, add dry white wine and reduce by half. Add the veal stock and reduce to required consistency. Pass through a fine sieve into clean pan and reserve.

To serve, carve the pork into thick slices, place on plates and coat with the sauce. Garnish with juniper berries and sage leaves.

HOBSON'S CHOICE
by **Harold Brighouse**
Old Vic 7 January 1964,
Director **John Dexter**
Willie **Frank Finlay**,
Maggie **Joan Plowright**,
Hobson **Michael Redgrave**

WILLIE There's nobbut tea to drink and I reckon what's in the pot is stewed, so I'll –

MAGGIE (taking pot off him as he moves to fireplace with it) You'll not do owt of sort. Father likes his liquids strong.

WILLIE A piece of pork pie now, Mr Hobson?

HOBSON (groaning) Pork pie!

MAGGIE (sharply) You'll be sociable now you're here, I hope. (She pours tea)

HOBSON It wasn't sociability that brought me, Maggie.

MAGGIE What was it then?

HOBSON Maggie, I'm in disgrace. A sore and sad misfortune's fallen on me.

MAGGIE (cutting) Happen a piece of wedding cake 'ull do you good.

HOBSON (shuddering) It's sweet.

MAGGIE That's natural in cake.

HOBSON I've gotten such a head.

MAGGIE Aye. But wedding cake's a question of heart. There'd be no bride cakes made at all if we thought first about our heads. I'm quite aware its foolishness, but I've a wish to see my father sitting at my table eating my wedding cake on my wedding day.

Veal Piccata with Mustard Sauce

Serves 4

12 x 2 oz (50g) veal piccata
1 oz (25g) butter
1 oz (25g) shallots, chopped
5 fl oz (150ml) dry white wine
10 fl oz (275ml) light veal stock
5 fl oz (150ml) double cream
half tablespoon coarse-grain mustard
salt
ground black pepper
tablespoon chopped chives
1 tomato, skinned, seeded and diced

Heat the butter in a pan and fry the veal in the butter, turning once. When cooked, remove from pan and keep warm. Add shallots to the pan, de-glaze with white wine and reduce by half, add the veal stock and reduce again. Whisk in the double cream and cook till consistency is smooth. Pass into a clean pan, blend in the mustard and season to taste.

To serve, flood the plates with mustard sauce and place veal pieces on top. Sprinkle with warm diced tomato and decorate with chopped chives.

THE CAPTAIN OF KÖPENICK
by **Carl Zuckmayer**
adapted by **John Mortimer**
Old Vic 9 March 1971,
Director **Frank Dunlop**
Von Schlettow **John Moffatt**

∘ Von SCHLETTOW Oh yes. It's all right for a fellow in uniform. In uniform I feel like a good fat, entrecôte steak, flared and rare. But in civvies I'm nothing but a small veal escalope, without mustard.

BLANQUETTE OF VEAL

Serves 4

1½ lbs (700g) diced lean veal
1 onion, studded with cloves &
bay leaf
1 carrot, peeled
2 sticks celery (tied with
string)
1 sprig thyme
salt
ground white pepper
1 pint (570ml) light veal stock
1½ oz (40g) flour
1½ oz (40g) butter
5 fl oz (150ml) double cream
1 tablespoon lemon juice
2 egg yolks
2 oz (50g) button onions,
peeled and cooked
2 oz (50g) button mushrooms,
wiped and cooked
1 tablespoon chopped parsley
2 slices de-crusted toast bread
2 oz (50g) butter

Place veal in a pan and cover with veal stock. Add the carrot, onion and celery and sprig of thyme. Lightly season, cover and bring to boil. Skim, lower heat and simmer, covered, till tender.

In another pan make the roux with butter and flour without browning. Drain the veal reserving the stock and keep the meat warm and moist. Add the stock to the roux gradually over low heat, stirring continuously to blend well. Cook for 5-10 minutes over low heat, stirring. Pass through a fine sieve into clean pan and reserve to one side.

Mix together in a bowl the egg yolks, cream and lemon juice and add this slowly to the hot but not boiling sauce. Add the veal, mushrooms and button onions to the sauce and heat gently to just under boiling point.

To serve, arrange on plates, sprinkle with chopped parsley and garnish with heart-shaped croutons made by frying the toast bread in butter and cutting with pastry cutter. Serve with buttered noodles or rice.

WRECKED EGGS
by **David Hare**
Cottesloe 9 September 1986 (with *The Bay at Nice*), Director **David Hare**
Robbie **Colin Stinton**,
Loelia **Kate Buffery**,
Grace **Zoë Wanamaker**

ROBBIE I lit the barbecue.

LOELIA Robbie, I've got a whole thing in the kitchen.

ROBBIE What d'you mean?

LOELIA Linguine. I've got soft-shell crabs marinating. And I've got veal. I'm making my blanquette.

ROBBIE (laughs) Oh no, I don't believe it. I went to the market this morning. While you were having a game. I got steaks. And Italian sausages. I was going to make cornbread.

LOELIA I can't believe it.

ROBBIE No, well it's true

(They are both laughing, delighted)

LOELIA That's wonderful.

ROBBIE Two dinners.

GRACE An excess of hospitality. An absence of guests.

ROBBIE Loelia's really an outstanding cook. (He is shaking his head, beaming at her.)

LOELIA I went to the New School croissant and brioche class. It costs forty dollars, but you get to keep what you make.

ROBBIE Boy, that was good. She used to come back to the apartment on a Saturday morning with what she'd just made. She did one which nearly made me faint. With cinnamon and raisins.

MEDALLIONS OF VEAL WITH LEMON SAUCE

Serves 4

8 x 2½ oz (65g) slices veal fillet
1 oz (25g) butter
1 oz (25g) shallot chopped
5 fl oz (150ml) double cream
4 fl oz (125ml) dry white wine
5 fl oz (150ml) veal stock
salt
ground white pepper
4 sprigs lemon balm
1 lemon
½ teaspoon sugar

Peel the zest from the lemon and cut into julienne strips. Put into a small saucepan with cold water to cover and bring to the boil. Drain, refresh in cold water, and drain again. Return the peel to the saucepan with the sugar and one tablespoon of water. Cook over a low heat until water has evaporated. Set aside and keep warm.

Segment the remaining lemon and keep to one side. Melt the butter in a pan and fry the veal pieces quickly on both sides. Remove and reserve. Add the shallots to the pan and cook till transparent. Add the dry white wine and any lemon juice left from segments. Reduce by half. Add the veal stock, salt and pepper and reduce again. Now add the double cream and thicken until coating consistency. Pass into a clean pan.

To serve, flood plates with sauce and arrange veal slices on top. Garnish with lemon segments, top with lemon zest and decorate with lemon balm.

ANTONY AND CLEOPATRA
by **William Shakespeare**
Olivier 9 April 1987, Director **Peter Hall**
Enobarbus **Michael Bryant**,
Maecenas **Graham Sinclair**

ENOBARBUS Ay, sir; we did sleep day out of countenance, and made the night light with drinking.

MAECENAS Eight wild boars roasted whole at a breakfast, and but twelve persons there; is this true?

VEAL STEAK WITH SAGE AND PARMA HAM

Serves 4

4 x 5 oz (150g) loin of veal
steaks
4 slices thin parma ham
8 sage leaves
1 tablespoon   olive oil
1 oz (25g) butter
4 fl oz (125ml) dry vermouth
4 fl oz (125ml) double cream
salt
ground black pepper
1 tablespoon chopped parsley

Place two sage leaves on each steak, season with black pepper and cover with the parma ham. Heat the butter and oil in a pan and place in the steak, ham side down. Fry until browned, turn and brown again until just cooked. Remove from pan and keep warm.

Add the vermouth to the pan and reduce until nearly evaporated. Add double cream and seasoning and reduce to desired consistency.

To serve, flood plates with the sauce, arrange veal steaks on plates, ham side up and sprinkle with chopped parsley.

H, or Monologues at Front of Burning Cities
by **Charles Wood**
Old Vic 13 February 1969,
Director **Geoffrey Reeves**
Captain Jones-Parry **Gerald James**

CAPTAIN JONES PARRY
Pigs will eat a body,

in Monmouth even,

a human body left lying where it

can be got at,

in poorer cases, it does sad to

say sometimes happen that your

Grannie ends up a Bath Chap.

Sirloin Steak with Stilton and Madeira Sauce

Serves 4

4 x 7 oz (200g) Scotch sirloin steaks
4 oz (125g) sliced Stilton
4 sprigs watercress
8 fl oz (225ml) strong beef stock
4 fl oz (125ml) madeira
1 oz (25g) butter
1 oz (25g) shallots, finely chopped
few crushed black peppercorns
1 sprig thyme
1 bay leaf
1 oz (25g) chilled butter, diced
salt
pepper

To make the sauce, melt 1 oz (25g) butter in a pan and add the shallots and cook until softened. Now add the black peppercorns, thyme and bayleaf and cook for a couple of minutes. Add madeira and reduce by half. Add the beef stock and reduce till syrupy texture.

Pass into a clean pan, heat gently and add the chilled butter piece by piece until sauce appears shiny. Reserve and keep warm.

Season and oil steaks and grill to desired stage. Place on tray, top with Stilton and place under grill until cheese melts.

To serve, flood plates with Madeira sauce, arrange steaks on plates and garnish with watercress.

PIANO
by **Trevor Griffiths**
Cottesloe, 8 August 1990,
Director **Howard Davies**
Triletski **Oliver Cotton**,
Anna **Penelope Wilton**

TRILETSKI Brilliantly put,
Sergei Pavolovich. And on the
subject of withering away, perhaps we could prevail upon our
good hostess to furnish a little
sustenance before too long. . .
I could eat a pig whole. Your
Excellency, I beg of you. . .

ANNA How impudent and tire-
some you have become,
Nikolai Ivanovich. Everyone
else waits, why shouldn't you?
How can you be hungry?
When are you ever not hungry? You spend your whole life
gorging yourself. This morning
what did you have, hunh? Two
glass of tea, a mound of beef,
five eggs . . .

TRILETSKI . . . Four . . .

ANNA Five, I watched you,
amazed. Then you stole into
the larder and demolished half
a pie. I've had no peace since
daybreak with your guzzling
and shouting.

THE PIED PIPER
by **Adrian Mitchell**
Music by **Dominic Muldowney**
Devised and directed by **Alan Cohen**
Based on the poem by **Robert Browning,** Olivier 11 November 1986, revived 4 November 1987
Egbert Saveloy **Bill Moody,**
Mayoress **Nicola Blackman,**
Baron Saveloy **Shaun Curry**

EGBERT Mum! I'm hungry, Mum!

MAYORESS I'm hungry too, my darling. I could eat a dinosaur.

BARON Where's me turtle soup? I don't feel like a Mayor without me turtle soup!

MAYORESS It's that new girl, Toffee. She's so slow.

BARON Where is that girl?

EGBERT Mum! I think I'm going to die of starvation!

(The SAVELOYS sing)

BARON Steaks by the score.

EGBERT Burgers galore.

MAYORESS I love the smell of meat, sir!

BARON Buckets of chips!

EGBERT Good for the hips!

MAYORESS Bring me a tower of pizza!

SAVELOYS Bring on the food
I'm in the mood
Bring on the jugs of vino
Nip down the pub
Get some more grub
We'll have a right old beano!

FILET MIGNON WITH WALNUT SAUCE

Serves 6

12 x 1 inch thick (2.5cm) slices
of beef fillet
4 sprigs watercress
8 fl oz (225ml) veal stock
2 fl oz (50ml) port
2 fl oz (50ml) red wine
1 oz (25g) shallot, finely
chopped
salt
pepper
1 fl oz (25ml) walnut oil
12 halved walnuts
12 walnuts, finely chopped
watercress to garnish

To make the sauce heat the walnut oil in pan, add the shallots and chopped walnuts and cook until softened. Add the red wine and port and reduce by half. Add the veal stock, season and reduce till syrupy texture.

Season and oil the slices of fillet and pan-fry over high heat until desired cooking stage. To serve arrange fillets on plates, coat with walnut sauce, decorate with watercress.

Roast Quail with Black Olives & Thyme

WHITE CHAMELEON
by **Christopher Hampton**
Cottesloe 14 February 1991,
Director **Richard Eyre**
Ibrahim **Saeed Jaffrey**,
Chris **David Birkin**

Serves 3

6 quails
2 oz (50g) butter
6 rashers back bacon
2 cloves garlic, peeled
12 sprigs thyme
18 black olives
4 fl oz (125ml) chicken stock
4 fl oz (125ml) white wine
1 tablespoon chopped parsley
6 sprigs watercress

Spread each quail with the butter and season. Lay one rasher of bacon across the breast of each bird and secure with string. Place the quails into a roasting tray with garlic, thyme and black olives arranged around them. Place into oven, gas mark 5 (375f°) (190°c) and cook for 10-15 minutes leaving slightly pink.

When cooked remove the quail from pan and keep warm. Tip off excess fat from pan, place on a high heat ring, deglaze with white wine and reduce till nearly evaporated. Add the chicken stock, season and reduce to desired consistency.

To serve, remove string from quail, arrange on plates, spoon over the saucepan contents and garnish with watercress and chopped parsley.

IBRAHIM Is very sad, the story of the quail.

CHRIS Why?

IBRAHIM He comes all the way from Europe, Italy, somewhere in Europe, across the sea, such a long way for a so small bird, all the way to Alexandria. So he is very tired, flying low. So we just put the nets, you see them on all the beaches this time in the year: and he flies into the net, bof, and falls on the ground. They just pick him, put him in the bag.

CHRIS It's cruel, they should catch them before they start.

IBRAHIM No, is like life, this way. Long journey, big struggle, then bof. Also, catch him first, he would be eaten by Italians.

CHRIS It's not fair, I don't think we ought to eat them.

IBRAHIM Yes, but is delicious.

102

PHEASANT CASSEROLE

Serves 4

2 small young pheasants
¾ pint (400ml) pheasant stock
salt
pepper
1 bouquet garni
1 oz (25g) flour
2 oz (50g) butter
4 fl oz (125ml) port
4 rashers rindless back bacon
4 oz (125g) button mushrooms
8 oz (225g) peeled chestnuts
4 heart-shaped croutons
1 tablespoon chopped parsley

Cut each pheasant into 4 portions. Put the giblets and the rest of the chopped pheasant carcase into a pan and cover with water. Add salt, pepper and bouquet garni. Bring to the boil, skim, reduce heat and simmer for 1 hour. When finished, strain and measure out ¾ pint (400ml) of stock and reserve.

Coat the pheasant joints in seasoned flour. Heat the butter in a large pan add the bacon and mushrooms and fry for 2-3 minutes. Remove from pan and place into casserole dish. Place the pheasant joints into the frying pan and fry until golden brown. Place into casserole with chestnuts.

Pour the reserved stock into the frying pan with the port, de-glaze and tip into the casserole. Cover tightly and cook in moderate oven, gas mark 4 (350°f) (180°c) for 1¼ hours. When cooked correct consistency and seasoning and serve garnished with heart-shaped croutons and chopped parsley.

TARTUFFE
by **Molière**
translated by **Richard Wilbur**
Old Vic 21 November 1967.
Director **Tyrone Guthrie**
Dorine **Joan Plowright,**
Orgon **John Gielgud**
(Jatinder Verma's version.
Director **Jatinder Verma**
Durgabai **Shelley King**,
Orgon **Ayub Khan Din**
Cottesloe 18 April 1990)

DORINE Your wife, two days ago, had a bad fever,
And a fierce headache which refused to leave her.

ORGON Ah. And Tartuffe?

DORINE Tartuffe? Why, he's round and red, .
Bursting with health, and excellently fed.

ORGON Poor fellow!

DORINE That night, the mistress was unable
To take a single bite at the dinner-table
Her headache-pains, she said, were simply hellish.

ORGON Ah. And Tartuffe?

DORINE He ate his meal with relish.
And zealously devoured in her presence
A leg of mutton and a brace of pheasants.

ORGON Poor fellow!

POT ROASTED GROUSE WITH HONEY

Serves 4

4 young grouse
4 oz (125g) butter
6 oz (175g) mixed carrot, leek, celery chopped
½ teaspoon chopped thyme
2 tablespoons honey
8 fl oz (225ml) dry cider
12 fl oz (350ml) chicken stock
4 fl oz (125ml) double cream
salt
pepper
watercress to garnish

Place half the butter in a heavy casserole dish, heat and add the vegetables and thyme and cook until soft. Add the grouse and coat the breast with the honey. Cover and cook in pre-heated oven gas mark 3 (325°f) (170°c) for one hour. Remove birds from casserole and keep them warm.

Pour the cider into the casserole, add chicken stock and deglaze over high heat ring. Skim and simmer until reduced by two-thirds, strain through a fine sieve into clean pan, raise heat, add the cream and simmer for a few minutes. Beat in the remaining butter till a nice glaze is achieved. Correct seasoning.

Arrange the grouse on four plates, garnish with watercress and serve the sauce separately.

BLITHE SPIRIT
by **Noël Coward**
Lyttelton 24 June 1976, Olivier 9 February 1977,
Director **Harold Pinter**
Mme Arcati **Elizabeth Spriggs**

MME ARCATI I can't go into trances at a moment's notice. It takes hours of preparation. In addition to which I have to be extremely careful of my diet for days beforehand. Today, for instance, I happened to lunch with friends and had pigeon pie which, plus these cucumber sandwiches, would make a trance out of the question.

Venison Pie

Serves 4

1 lb (450g) puff pastry
1½ lbs (700g) diced stewing venison
1 bouquet garni
salt
pepper
10 crushed juniper berries
8 fl oz (225ml) red wine
2 fl oz (50ml) port
1 clove garlic, crushed
2 medium onions, diced
4 oz (125g) button mushrooms
4 rashers rindless back bacon, diced
½ pint (275ml) game stock
1 oz (25g) flour
1 oz (25g) lard
1 beaten egg

Place venison in a deep stainless steel bowl, pour over the red wine and port, add the bouquet garni, garlic and juniper berries. Cover and leave to marinate in refrigerator for 48 hours.

Strain the venison, reserving marinade. Melt the fat in a pan, add the venison and flour and brown. Remove from pan and place in casserole dish. Add to the pan the diced bacon, onions and mushrooms and cook till softened. Strain the marinade into the pan and reduce by half. Add the game stock, boil, skim and reduce again. Correct seasoning and pour into casserole. Cover and cook in oven, gas mark 3 (325°f) (170°c) for 2 hours.

When cooked place into pie dish and leave to cool. Cover with puff pastry, brush with the beaten egg and bake in hot oven gas mark 7 (425°f) (220°c) for 20-25 minutes until pastry has risen. Then lower the heat to gas mark 4 (350°f) (180°c) and cook for a further 10 minutes.

MURMURING JUDGES
by **David Hare**
Olivier, 10 October 1991,
Director **Richard Eyre**
Rt Hon Kevin Cumberland **Peter Wight**,
Justice Cuddeford **Michael Bryant**,
Sir Peter Edgecombe QC **Richard Pasco**

(Kevin picks up a menu-card from the table)

KEVIN "Roast Venison Baden-Baden". Just exactly how is that done?

(Cuddeford smiles)

CUDDEFORD I think you'll find it's a young roebuck.

KEVIN Ah yes.

CUDDEFORD It's been shot through the heart and then skinned. Then basted in some sort of fruity, substantial gravy.

KEVIN Good gracious.

CUDDEFORD Then it's served up to us. (He smiles. The HOME SECRETARY watches him, a little bemused, but too old a hand to let himself show it) As you know we have a system whereby law students have to eat dinners to qualify.

KEVIN I've heard that.

CUDDEFORD They have to eat their way through forty dinners a year. We were proposing to abolish this requirement as outdated. But then we found that without this, so to speak, ready-made pool of captive consumers, the entire kitchen effort would not be economic.

KEVIN That's tricky.

CUDDEFORD Hence we would not be able to give ourselves lunch.

(The HOME SECRETARY looks to Sir PETER)

SIR PETER It's true.

CUDDEFORD And that of course would be catastrophic.

Rump Steak and Oyster Pie

Serves 4

1 lb (450g) puff pastry
1½ lbs (700g) diced, lean rump
steak
seasoned flour
2 oz (50g) butter
4 oz (125g) button mushrooms
2 oz (50g) chopped onions
½ pint (275ml) beef stock
4 fl oz (125ml) red wine
1 teaspoon chopped thyme
1 tablespoon Worcestershire
sauce
salt
pepper
8 large oysters
1 beaten egg

Roll the beef in seasoned flour. Melt the butter in a pan and sauté the oysters until firm to touch. Remove and leave to one side.

Add the beef to the pan and brown. Remove and set to one side.

Add the chopped onion to the pan with the button mushrooms and chopped thyme and cook for a few minutes. Return the steak to the mixture, add the red wine and Worcestershire sauce. Cook for a further few minutes, then add beef stock. Cover and cook over low heat till tender. Correct consistency by reducing. Season and cool.

Place into pie dish, top with oysters and cover with puff pastry. Brush with beaten egg and cook in oven gas mark 7 (425°f) (220°c) for 10-15 minutes, then lower heat to gas mark 4 (350°f) (180°c) and cook for a further 5 minutes. Serve immediately.

ON THE RAZZLE
by **Tom Stoppard**
adapted from **Johann Nestroy**
Lyttelton 22 September 1981,
Director **Peter Wood**
Melchior **Michael Kitchen**,
Zangler **Dinsdale Landen**

MELCHIOR The ploughman's lunch is six oysters and a crème de menthe frappé.

ZANGLER I see... well, perhaps just this once.

MELCHIOR Leave it to me, sir – champagne – lobster – roast fowl – birthday cake.

ZANGLER Birthday cake – pickles – dumplings -

MELCHIOR And to finish off, to get her in the mood -

ZANGLER Perhaps we should have -

MELCHIOR+ZANGLER [together] A nice bottle of the hard stuff.

MELCHIOR [leaving] Schnapps!

SHEPHERD'S PIE

Serves 4

1 lb (450g) cooked minced lamb
2 finely chopped onions
3 oz (75g) unsalted butter
6 oz (175g) lamb stock
1 tablespoon tomato purée
1 teaspoon Worcestershire sauce
salt
pepper
2 fl oz (50ml) milk
1 lb (450g) mashed potato
chopped parsley to garnish

Cook the onions in 1 oz (25g) of the butter until soft. Add the meat and cook until browned. Stir in the stock, tomato purée, Worcestershire sauce and seasoning.

Beat the remaining melted butter and milk into the mashed potatoes. Place the meat into a greased ovenproof dish, cover with potato and decorate the top with a fork. Bake in a hot oven gas mark 7 (425°f) (220°c) for 30 minutes or until potato browns.

Serve the pie hot, sprinkled with chopped parsley.

THE SECRET RAPTURE
by **David Hare**
Lyttelton 4 October 1988,
Director **Howard Davies**
Isobel **Jill Baker**,
Katherine **Clare Higgins**

KATHERINE sits down on a small wooden chair. ISOBEL comes in with a hot dish between oven gloves. She sets it down on the table.

ISOBEL I only said it would be nice to go for a walk.

KATHERINE Well, it wouldn't be nice.

ISOBEL No, plainly.

KATHERINE What's this?

ISOBEL Shepherd's pie.

(KATHERINE looks up at her)

KATHERINE Are you out of your mind?

ISOBEL Eat

KATHERINE Your cooking is unspeakable. It's all good intentions. Fuck shepherd's pie. It sums you up.

(ISOBEL takes no notice, just helps herself to some. KATHERINE watches with distaste)

All right, let's go out. Let's go to a French restaurant.

ISOBEL Don't be ridiculous.

CASSOULET

HALF-LIFE

by **Julian Mitchell**
Cottesloe 17 November 1977, West
End from 2 March 1978.
Director **Waris Hussein**.
Noel **John Gielgud**,
Jones **Paul Rogers**

NOEL (sniffing) It's not ... I
don't detect cassoulet in the
air, do I? You're not giving us
cassoulet?

JONES I'm not giving you
anything if you don't get
dressed.

NOEL Oh, don't nanny me!
Are we having cassoulet or
not?

JONES Are you getting
dressed?

NOEL Not till you tell me.

JONES Then, no, captain. We
are not having cassoulet.

Serves 4

2 duck legs
4 best end of lamb chops
8 oz (225g) spicy sausage
2 oz (50g) onions, sliced
1 stick celery, chopped
4 cloves garlic, crushed
12 oz (350g) haricot beans soaked in water for 4-5 hours
salt
ground black pepper
8 oz (225g) tomatoes, skinned, seeded and chopped
2 bay leaves
1 pint (570ml) chicken stock
2 oz (50g) fresh white breadcrumbs

Trim any excess fat from the meat and cut sausage into large chunks. Layer the meat, beans and vegetables in a large earthenware pot, lightly seasoning each layer. Place the tomatoes on top with the bay leaf. Pour on stock, cover, and cook in oven, gas mark 3 (325°f) (170°c) for 2½ hours.

Remove from the oven, stir the cassoulet and sprinkle with breadcrumbs. Raise the oven temperature and put back into oven, uncovered, until topping is brown and crisp. Sprinkle with chopped parsley and take casserole dish to the table.

DESSERTS

Pink Grapefruit and Vermouth Sorbet

Serves 6–8

32 fl oz (920ml) pink
grapefruit juice
6 oz (175g) icing sugar
4 fl oz (125ml) dry vermouth
2 large egg whites
4 sprigs mint

Blend the fruit juice with the sugar and pour into freezer-proof container. Freeze until frozen 1 inch (2.5cm) around the edges (about one hour). Remove from freezer, add vermouth, place in liquidizer and blend till smooth.

Replace in freezer and freeze to a firm slush (about 2 hours).

Beat the egg whites till stiff but not dry. Take out the fruit mixture, fold into the water ice gently and freeze again for 3-4 hours.

To serve, take out sorbet for a few minutes to soften, serve in chilled glass, garnished with mint sprig.

SINGLE SPIES
by **Alan Bennett**
Lyttelton 1 December 1988
(West End from February 1989).
Directors **Alan Bennett & Simon Callow**
Coral **Prunella Scales**,
Burgess **Simon Callow**
From *An Englishman Abroad*

CORAL What is that smell?

BURGESS Me probably.

CORAL No. Besides that. If it's our lunch, it's burning.

BURGESS Oh. Now. It might be.

(He gets up unhurriedly and goes into the kitchenette)

Yes, it is. It was stew.

(He peers into the pan)

One could salvage some of it?

(He shows it to Coral)

CORAL Hardly.

BURGESS Perhaps not.

(He returns to the kitchen with it)

However. All is not lost. I managed to scrounge two tomatoes this morning, and quite a talking point, a grapefruit. Shall we perch? I generally do.

CORAL (faintly) Treats.

(He puts a tomato on her plate and eats his like an apple)

BURGESS Garlic?

CORAL No thank you.

BURGESS I love it.

(He eats several cloves)

Yum yum. Now. Tell me all the gossip. Do you see Harold Nicolson?

Apple, Apricot and Calvados Mousse

Serves 6–8

8 oz (225g) dried apricots, soaked overnight
1 lb (450g) cooking apples
zest of ½ lemon
juice of ½ lemon
½ oz (10g) powdered gelatine
2 large eggs, separated
3 oz (75g) sugar
5 fl oz (150ml) lightly whipped cream
1 measure Calvados
whipped cream
toasted almonds

Drain the soaked apricots, reserving liquid, and measure 10 fl oz of soaking liquid into a pan. Add the apricots. Peel and core the apples, chop coarsely and add to the pan with lemon zest and juice and Calvados. Heat the pan gently for 20 minutes until apricots are soft.

Sprinkle the gelatine with a little water, leave till the liquid is absorbed. Heat the gelatine until dissolved.

In a bowl beat the egg yolks lightly. Put the fruit into a blender and purée. Blend the egg yolks with the fruit purée and sweeten to taste with sugar. Add gelatine. Make up the purée to 1½ pints (850ml) with water. Put in a bowl and stir over crushed ice until point of setting.

In another bowl whisk egg whites until they hold their shape in soft peaks. With a large metal spoon fold the whipped cream into the fruit purée followed by the egg whites. Pour the mixture into wetted moulds and set in refrigerator.

To serve, dip moulds into hot water, turn onto plates decorate with whipped cream and toasted almonds.

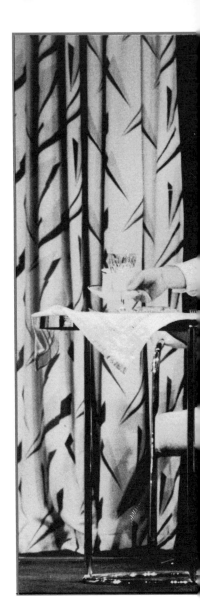

ROUGH CROSSING

by **Tom Stoppard**
adapted from *Play at the Castle* by **Ferenc Molnar**
Lyttelton 30 October 1984,
Director **Peter Wood**
Dvornichek **Michael Kitchen,**
Turai **John Standing**

DVORNICHEK Will you be requiring early morning tea, sir?

TURAI Yes.

DVORNICHEK What time?

TURAI What time is it now?

DVORNICHEK Coming up to one o'clock.

TURAI I'll have it at half past one, three o'clock, four thirty and six.

DVORNICHEK With milk or lemon?

TURAI With cognac. Breakfast at seven.

DVORNICHEK Yes, sir. Tea or coffee?

TURAI Black coffee. Half a grapefruit. Perhaps a little ham ... sausage, scrambled eggs,

kidneys, a potato, or two ... some cold cuts – chicken, beef, tongue, salami – oh, some kind of smoked fish, I'm not fussy – cheese, white rolls, brown toast, a couple of croissants, butter, strawberry jam, honey, pancakes and some stewed fruit.

DVORNICHEK Cream?

TURAI (sharply) No. (Then relenting) Well, a little. I only eat once a day.

ICED CAPUCCINO MOUSSE

Serves 8

6-7 oz (170-200g) sugar
5 egg yolks
3 egg whites, stiffly beaten
1 pint (570ml) whipped cream
1 tablespoon coffee essence

Mix egg yolks with sugar. Place in top part of double boiler and heat slowly, whipping all the time. When the mixture thickens, remove from the heat and continue beating until quite cold. Add coffee essence, stiffly beaten egg whites, and whipped cream.

Pour into large coffee cups to serve, sprinkled with cocoa powder.

TWELFTH NIGHT
by **William Shakespeare**
Old Vic Mobile 4 January 1973,
Director **Peter James**
Sir Toby Belch **David Bauer**,
Sir Andrew Aguecheek **David Bradley**

SIR TOBY: Does not our life consist of the four elements?

SIR ANDREW: Faith, so they say; but, I think, it rather consists of eating and drinking.

PURE GENIUS MOUSSE

Serves 4–6

10 oz (275g) bitter chocolate
3 eggs, separated
¾ pint (400ml) whipping cream
1 leaf gelatine

Cut the chocolate into small pieces and place in bowl. Whisk the egg whites into peaks. Soak the gelatine in cold water.

Whisk ½ pint (275ml) of the cream to soft peaks. Melt the chocolate in a bowl over simmering water. Remove from heat and gently mix in the egg yolk and softened gelatine. Fold in the cream, then the egg whites and mix until smooth and combined.

Divide into glasses, allow to chill for 30 minutes and top with the remaining cream lightly whipped.

MAN, BEAST AND VIRTUE
by **Luigi Pirandello**
adapted by **Charles Wood**
Cottesloe 7 September 1989,
Director **William Gaskill**
Paolino **Trevor Eve**,
Toto **William Hoyland**

(Toto has made a cake containing aphrodisiac to ensure that the Captain will sleep with his wife and legitimise Paolino's baby, which she is carrying)

PAOLINO What is that?

TOTO Chocolate and cream gateau, very nice. Delicious. Scrumptious.

PAOLINO Don't try to tempt me you fool. This isn't a bloody party for me.

TOTO I had to make it. Look. (TOTO opens the box, shows PAOLINO) . . couldn't have cakes, little fingers picking up cakes . . . see, there can be no mistake, half white, half chocolate, it's in the chocolate. The boy may have the white half, and you if you want some. It's the chocolate he must eat.

PAOLINO Chocolate for the Captain. Will it . . . ?

TOTO Oh yes, yes, yes, yes! Fear not.

MANGO FOOL

Serves 4

1 large ripe mango, peeled and
chopped
1 fl oz (25ml) thick Greek
yoghurt
3 fl oz (75ml) double cream
1 oz (25g) icing sugar

Place the chopped mango
in a food processor and
purée. Add the yoghurt,
double cream and sugar and
blend till stiff. Pour into glasses
and chill, serve garnished with
mango slices.

AMERICAN BUFFALO
by David Mamet
Cottesloe 28 June 1978, Revival 5
October 1978, Director **Bill Bryden**
Walter Cole (Teacher) **Jack Shepherd**,
Donny Dubrow **Dave King**

TEACH You shouldn't eat that
shit.

DON Why?

TEACH It's just I have a feel-
ing about healthfoods

DON It's not healthfoods,
Teach. It's only yoghurt.

TEACH That's not health-
foods?

DON No. They've had it
forever.

TEACH Yoghurt?

DON Yeah. They used to joke
about it on My Little Margie (To
Bob) Way before your time.

TEACH Yeah?

DON Yeah.

TEACH What the fuck. A little
bit can't hurt you.

RASPBERRY FOOL

AMARETTO SYLLABUB

Serves 4

1 lb (450g) fresh raspberries
1 measure crème de cassis
4 fl oz (125ml) double cream
1 oz (25g) icing sugar
4 mint leaves to garnish

Serves 6

3 fl oz (75ml) Amaretto liqueur
2 tablespoons lemon juice
3 oz (75g) castor sugar
10 fl oz (275ml) double cream
amaretto biscuits for garnish

Place the amaretto, lemon juice and sugar in a bowl and leave till sugar dissolves. Add the fresh cream and whip until softly stiff and holds shape. Transfer to glass dishes and chill. Serve with crushed Amaretto biscuits on top.

Place the raspberries and crème de cassis in a blender and purée till smooth. Pass through a fine sieve to remove pips. Return to blender, add the double cream and icing sugar and beat till stiff.

Pour into glasses and chill, garnish with reserved whole raspberry and mint leaf.

AMADEUS
by **Peter Shaffer**
Olivier 2 November 1979
Director **Peter Hall**
Salieri **Paul Scofield**

SALIERI It's a little repellent, I admit – but actually the first sin I have to confess to you is Gluttony. Sticky gluttony at that. Infantine – Italian gluttony! The truth is that all my life I have never been able to conquer a lust for the sweetmeats of northern Italy where I was born. From the ages of three to seventy-three my entire career has been conducted to the taste of almonds sprinkled with sifted sugar. (Lustfully) Veronese biscuits! Milanese macaroons! Snow dumplings with pistachio sauce! (Pause) Do not judge me too harshly for this. All men harbour patriotic feelings of some kind.

LIME SYLLABUB

WHISKY SYLLABUB

Serves 6

5 fl oz (150ml) dry white wine
2 tablespoons lime juice
2 level teaspoons grated lime zest
3 oz (75g) castor sugar
10 fl oz (275ml) double cream
lime slices for garnish

Place the wine, lime juice, zest and sugar in a bowl and leave till sugar dissolves. Add the fresh cream and whip until the mixture is softly stiff and holds its shape.

Transfer to serving glasses and chill. Garnish with lime slices.

Serves 6

6 tablespoons thin shredded marmalade
1 oz (25g) castor sugar
2½ fl oz (60ml) whisky
juice of 1 lemon
10 fl oz (275ml) double cream

Mix together the marmalade, sugar, whisky, and lemon juice. Whip the cream until softly stiff and whisk in the marmalade mixture until the cream stands in soft peaks.

Serve in small whisky tumblers garnished with marmalade rind.

BLACKCURRANT AND CASSIS JELLY, SERVED WITH FROMAGE FRAIS

Serves 6

2 lb (900g) fresh picked
blackcurrants
8 oz (225g) castor sugar
5 fl oz (150ml) crème de cassis
1 oz (25g) leaf gelatine
fromage frais

Place the blackcurrants in a pan with ½ pint (275ml) of water and the sugar. Heat and bring to the boil and simmer until soft. Cool. Strain the blackcurrants and pass through fine sieve. Return sieved blackcurrant pulp to the juice, add the crème de cassis and make the liquid up to two pints (1.1 litres) with water if necessary.

Soak the gelatine in 2 fl oz (50ml) of water until soft. Place in pan and dissolve over a low heat and pour into the blackcurrant mixture. Mix thoroughly. Place into 6 wetted moulds of desired shape and chill until set.

When set remove by placing in hot water for a few seconds. Turn onto plate and garnish with fromage frais and blackcurrants.

WHEN WE ARE MARRIED
by **J B Priestley**
Lyttelton 12 December 1979,
Director **Robin Lefevre**
Ruby **Mary Maddox**,
Gerald **John Quayle**

RUBY You'll have to wait, 'cos they haven't finished their tea.

GERALD Bit late, aren't they?

RUBY It's a do.

GERALD It's what?

RUBY A do. Y'know, they've company

GERALD Oh – I see. It's a sort of party, and they're having high tea.

RUBY Roast pork, stand pie, salmon and salad, trifle, two kinds o' jellies, lemon-cheese tarts, jam tarts, Swiss tarts, sponge cake, walnut cake, chocolate roll, and a pound cake kept from last Christmas.

GERALD Is that all?

RUBY No, there's white bread, brown bread, currant teacake, one o' them big curd tarts from Gregory's, and a lot o' cheese.

GERALD It is a do, isn't it?

RUBY And a little brown jug.

GERALD A little brown jug?

RUBY You know what that is, don't you? Don't you? (she laughs) Well, I never did! Little brown jug's a drop o' rum for your tea. They're getting right lively on it.

PEACH MELBA

Serves 4

2 large peaches
8 oz (225g) fresh raspberries
2 oz (50g) castor sugar
15 fl oz (400ml) home-made
vanilla ice cream

Put the peaches in a bowl and cover with boiling water. Leave for no more than one minute. Drain and peel. Cut the peaches in half and carefully remove the stones. Place to one side.

Rub the raspberries through a fine sieve into a mixing bowl and sweeten with the sugar.

To serve, place two scoops of vanilla ice cream in each glass, top with one peach half, round side up and spoon over raspberry purée. Serve immediately.

A FLEA IN HER EAR
by **Georges Feydeau**
translated by **John Mortimer**
Old Vic 8 February 1966,
Director **Jacques Charon**
Feraillon **Michael Turner**,
Finache **Kenneth Mackintosh**

FERAILLON Didn't you ever hear of the beautiful Castana? Her they used to call "The Copper-Bottomed Contessa"..?

FINACHE The name's familiar ...

FERAILLON She was the Duc de Choisel's mistress – for many years.

FINACHE Wasn't there a Freemason's Dinner, where she was served up stark naked with the Pêche Melba? On a silver plate – with sponge fingers!

FERAILLON You've hit it! That's her. That's my wife! I married her

VANILLA POACHED PEAR

RASPBERRY BAVAROIS

Serves 4

4 large ripe pears
½ pint (275ml) white wine
4 oz (125g) castor sugar
1 vanilla pod
rind of 1 lemon

Put the wine, sugar, vanilla pod and lemon rind together into a deep saucepan. Bring slowly to the boil. Peel the pears and core from the bottom. Place into the hot syrup, bring rapidly to the boil and boil for 5 minutes.

Reduce the heat and simmer gently until pears are transparent looking and soft. If the syrup is thin, remove the pears and boil the liquid fast until desired consistency is reached.

Allow pears to cool in syrup and serve in glass bowls surrounded with syrup and fresh double cream.

Serves 8

½ lb (225g) fresh raspberries
6oz (170g) icing sugar
juice of ½ lemon
½ oz (14g) leaf gelatine
½ pt (275ml) whipped cream
2½ fl oz (70ml) water

Reserve a few raspberries for decoration. Sieve the rest through a hair sieve and mix with the sugar and the juice of half a lemon. Soak the gelatine and dissolve in water at just above blood heat. Mix with the purée and stir well. Let the purée cool. As soon as it starts to set, fold in the whipped cream and pour into a mould.

To serve, decorate with whipped cream and whole raspberries.

Marsala Sabayon Mousse

Serves 6

12 yolks of egg
3 fl oz (75ml) Marsala
5 oz (150g) sugar
3 fl oz (75ml) whipped cream
2 oz castor sugar
3 candied cherries
3 oz (75g) grated chocolate

Beat egg yolks, Marsala and sugar together. Put in a double saucepan and beat until mixture thickens. Continue stirring as it cools. Pour into dishes and place in the fridge.

Beat the cream and castor sugar, and use this to decorate. Place half a cherry on top and the grated chocolate, and serve.

DANCING AT LUGHNASA
by **Brian Friel**
Lyttelton 15 October 1990.
Director **Patrick Mason**
Maggie **Anita Reeves**,
Chris **Catherine Byrne**

MAGGIE She's home safe and sound and that's all that matters. Now I don't know about you girls but I can tell you this chicken is weak with hunger. Let me tell you what's on the menu this evening. Our beverage is the usual hot, sweet tea. There is a choice between wheaten bread and soda-bread, both fresh from the chef's oven. But now we come to the difficulty: there are only three eggs between the seven of us – I wish to God you'd persuade that white rooster of yours to lay eggs, Rosie.

CHRIS There are eight of us, Maggie.

MAGGIE How are there – ? Of course – the soldier up the sycamore! Not a great larder but a nice challenge to someone like myself. Right. My suggestion is . . . Eggs Ballybeg; in other words scrambled and served on lightly toasted wheaten bread. Followed – for those so inclined – by one magnificent Wild Woodbine. Everybody happy?

Almond Blancmange

Strawberry Romanoff

Serves 8
4 oz (125g) ground almonds
5 fl oz (150ml) milk
4 oz (125g) castor sugar
2 leaves gelatine, dissolved
8 fl oz (225ml) double cream, whipped
brandy to taste
sugared almonds for garnish

Bring the milk to the boil in a thick bottomed pan. Remove from heat, add ground almonds and sugar. Return to low heat for 2 minutes.

Remove from heat, transfer to a clean bowl and add dissolved leaf gelatine. Cool. When mixture begins to set, fold in double whipped cream. Add the brandy to taste.

Spoon into individual ramekins and chill. To serve, place ramekin on plate garnished with sugared almonds.

Serves 6

1 lb (450g) strawberries
juice of 1 orange
2 fl oz (50ml) Curaçao
10 fl oz (275ml) double cream
3 oz (75g) castor sugar

Steep the strawberries in the orange juice and Curaçao. Place in an iced bowl and decorate with Chantilly cream (double cream whipped together with castor sugar) piped through a forcing bag with fluted nozzle

GAELIC COFFEE TRIFLE

Serves 6

1 packet of trifle sponges
2 tablespoons coffee essence
4 tablespoons whisky
3 oz (75g) castor sugar
3 oz (75g) cornflour
1 pint (570ml) milk
1 oz (25g) English butter
10 fl oz (275ml) fresh double cream
6 walnut halves
2 egg yolks

Put the trifle sponges into a glass bowl. Mix half the coffee essence with 3 tablespoons of whisky and pour over the sponges.

Place the sugar, cornflour and milk in a saucepan. Mix well. Heat gently, stirring continuously with a wooden spoon, until the sauce thickens and boils. Cook gently for 3 minutes. Remove from the heat and stir in the egg yolks and remaining coffee essence. Cook for a further one minute and remove from heat again. Mix in the butter and remaining whisky. Cool.

Whip the cream until stiff and fold half into the coffee mixture and spoon over the trifle sponges. Decorate with remaining whipped cream and walnut halves.

SNOW DUMPLINGS

Serves 8

1 pint (570ml) milk
½ pint (275ml) single cream
3 teaspoons castor sugar
1 teaspoon vanilla essence
3 teaspoons cornflour
6 egg yolks beaten
4 egg whites
pinch of salt
5 oz (150g) castor sugar
1 oz (25g) chopped almonds

Slowly bring half the milk to the boil with the cream, sugar (3 teaspoons) and vanilla essence. In a bowl, mix the cornflour with a little water, then add a little of the milk mixture onto the cornflour and stir well. Pour back into the milk mixture and bring to the boil, gently stirring continuously with wooden spoon. Simmer for 4 minutes.

Place the beaten egg yolks in another bowl and add the milk mixture beating all the time. This should become thick enough to coat the back of a spoon. Strain this custard into a shallow dish and allow to cool.

Heat the remaining milk in a deep frying pan with a pint (570ml) of water until simmering. Meanwhile whisk egg whites with salt until stiff. Gradually fold in the 5 oz (150g) of sugar until very smooth. Cook spoonfuls of meringue mixture in the simmering milk for no more than 30 seconds on each side. Lift out with perforated spoon and drain on absorbent cloth. Cool.

To serve, flood plates with custard mixture, place on the meringue dumplings and sprinkle with chopped almonds.

CRÈME BRÛLÉE

Serves 6

1 pint (570ml) fresh whipping cream
4 egg yolks
3 oz (75g) castor sugar
1 teaspoon vanilla essence

Put the fresh cream in top part of double boiler and heat gently, but do not boil. Meanwhile put the egg yolks, 2 oz (50g) of the castor sugar and vanilla essence into a mixing bowl and beat together. To this add the warmed cream and mix together.

Pour the mixture into six individual ramekin dishes and place in roasting tin, filled with enough water to come half way up side of dishes. Bake in the oven at gas mark 2 (300°f) (150°c) for about 1 hour or until set.

When cooked remove from roasting tin and leave to go cold. Chill in refrigerator overnight.

Sprinkle the top of each crème brûlée with the remaining sugar. Put under pre-heated hot grill until the sugar turns to caramel. Chill for 2-3 hours before serving.

COUNTING THE WAYS

by **Edward Albee**
Olivier 6 December 1976,
Director **Bill Bryden**
She **Beryl Reid**, He **Michael Gough**

(SHE enters, sucking a finger, a dishrag over one arm.)

SHE (Quite businesslike, if a trifle preoccupied) Walnuts. Parsley. Bone Marrow. Celery root (Suspicious) Do you love me?

HE (Pause; HE, too, suspicious) What happened to the Crème Brûlée?

SHE (flat) There's no Crème Brûlée.

HE· What do you mean there's no Crème Brûlée.

SHE (As before) There's no Crème Brûlée.

HE (Pause) There's always Crème Brûlée.

SHE Not today. (Pause; uncertain) Do you love me?

HE (Pause; shrugs; some distaste) Sure. (Pause; not too friendly) What happened?

SHE (Sits; dispirited) You know that lovely caramel that coats the Crème Brûlée.

HE Yes! Yum-yum!

SHE You know it. You know how it's done: the sugar, the maple sugar is sprinkled over the lovely custards – remember the lovely custards?

HE Yes! Yum-yum!

SHE And popped into the oven, so to caramelize.

HE Yum-yum!

SHE And then, at the end, into the broiler; under the broiler for a little, so the sugar crusts – that lovely crust you love.

HE Yes!

SHE Under the broiler for just a moment, just enough. It is not the time to straighten up, look out the window, unfocus

your eyes on some distant spot and daydream – ruminate; think.

HE Certainly not!

SHE For if you do that, your caramel will scorch, or worse: will blacken, become hard, burned and awful!

HE Ugh!

SHE There is nothing for it then but to throw it all away . . .

HE I should think so!

SHE The pan as well.

HE (Long pause; quiet tone) I see. Well. Indeed.

SHE (Sighs heavily) So that is why . . .

HE (A sad soft truth) . . . there is no Crème Brûlée.

SHE (Suspicious) Do you love me?

HE (Very grudging; coarse tone) Yeah.

SHE (Apologetic) I can make you something else.

HE (Rather cool) Yeah? What?

SHE (Straining for forgiveness) What would you like?

HE (Heavy) We got any pans left?

SHE (Soft) Be nice.

HE How about . . . how about that other thing you make . . . that, uh . . . Idiot's Delight, or whatever you call it?

SHE (Pause, 'til it comes to her) Raspberry Fool!! Oh! Yes; well, all right!

HE (Brightening) I like that.

SHE (Stands; brightens) Raspberry Fool it is! (SHE starts toward the exit, pauses; tentative again) Will you love me?

HE (Looks up; big smile) You bet!

BLACKOUT

Summer Pudding with Chantilly Cream

Serves 4–6

6 large slices of stale white
bread
4 oz (125g) sugar
1½ lb (700g) soft summer fruit
(either raspberries,
strawberries, stoned cherries,
blackcurrants, red currants or a
mixture)
½ egg white

5 fl oz (150ml) cream
1 oz (30g) icing sugar, sifted
vanilla essence

Remove the crusts from the bread. Cut into neat fingers.

Put the sugar and 5 table-spoons water into a pan and heat slowly, stirring, until the sugar dissolves. Add the fruit and simmer gently for about 7–10 minutes.

Line the base and sides of a 2 pint (1.1 litre) pudding basin with bread fingers and half the hot fruit mixture. Cover with more bread fingers. Pour in the rest of the fruit mixture and top with the remaining bread fingers. Cover with a saucer or plate. Place a heavy weight on top. Refrigerate or leave in a cold place overnight.

To make Chantilly cream, whip the fresh cream until softly stiff and fold in the icing sugar and a few drops of vanilla essence. Chill well until required. Turn the pudding onto a plate and serve with the Chantilly cream.

SALOME
by **Oscar Wilde**
Lyttelton 7 November 1989,
Director **Steven Berkoff**
Herod **Steven Berkoff**,
Salome **Katharine Schlesinger**

HEROD Bring me ripe fruits.
(Fruits are brought) Salomé,
come and eat fruit with me. I
love to see in a fruit the mark
of thy little teeth. Bite but a little
of this fruit and then I will eat
what is left.

SALOME I am not hungry,
Tetrarch.

QUEEN OF PUDDINGS

Serves 4

4 eggs
1 pint (570ml) milk
4 oz (125g) fine white breadcrumbs
4 tablespoons raspberry jam
3 oz (75g) castor sugar

Separate 3 eggs and beat together, in a bowl, the 3 egg yolks and one whole egg. Add to the milk and mix well. Then add the breadcrumbs.

Put the jam on the bottom of a pie dish about ½ inch (1 cm) thick, pour over the milk and egg mixture and leave for 30 minutes. Bake in the oven, gas mark 2 (300°f) (150°c) for 1 hour until set.

Now whisk the egg whites until stiff and fold in the sugar. Place the meringue mixture on top of the set custard, sprinkle with a little sugar and return to a cool oven for a further 15 minutes, until the meringue is set and browned.

CHERRY BATTER PUDDING

Serves 6

3 tablespoons flour
3 eggs beaten
5 tablespoons castor sugar
15 fl oz (400ml) milk
1 tablespoon rum
2 oz (50g) butter
1½lb(700g) stoned black
cherries
pinch of salt

Sift the flour and salt into a bowl, blend in the eggs and add 3 tablespoons sugar. Heat the milk until luke warm, add the rum and stir into the egg mixture until smooth.

Butter a shallow dish, put in the cherries, pour in the batter and dot with the remaining butter. Bake in the oven gas mark 7 (425°f) (220°c) for 25-30 minutes.

Sprinkle the pudding with the remaining sugar and serve warm.

THE CHERRY ORCHARD
by **Anton Chekhov**
Translator **Ronald Hingley**
Old Vic 24 May 1973,
Director **Michael Blakemore**
Firs **Harry Lomax**, Gayev **Michael Hordern**, Ranevskaya **Constance Cummings**, Pishchik **Kenneth Mackintosh**
Michael Frayn translation, Olivier 14 February 1978, Director **Peter Hall**
Firs **Ralph Richardson/Robin Bailey**, Gayev **Robert Stephens**, Ranevskaya **Dorothy Tutin**, Pishchik **Terence Rigby**
Mike Alfreds/Lilia Sokolov translation, Cottesloe 10 December 1985, Director **Mike Alfreds**
Firs **Hugh Lloyd**, Gayev **Edward Petherbridge**, Ranevskaya **Sheila Hancock**, Pishchik **Roy Kinnear**

FIRS In the old days, forty or fifty years ago, the cherries used to be dried, preserved and bottled. They used to make jam out of them, and time was –

GAYEV Be quiet please, Firs.

FIRS Time was when dried cherries used to be sent to Moscow and Kharkob by the wagon-load. They fetched a lot of money. Soft and juicy those dried cherries were, sweet and tasty. People had the knack of it in those days. The recipe –

RANEVSKY But where's the recipe now?

FIRS Forgotten. No one remembers it.

PISHCHIK (to Madame RANEVSKY) How are things in Paris, eh? Eat any frogs?

RANEVSKY I ate crocodiles.

PISHCHIK Extraordinary thing.

CABINET PUDDING

Serves 4

6 trifle sponges
2 oz (50g) glacé cherries, coarsely chopped
1 oz (25g) castor sugar
2 eggs
1 pint (570ml) milk
1 teaspoon vanilla essence
double cream to serve

Cut each sponge into 6 cubes. Put into a bowl with the cherries and sugar. Beat together the eggs, milk and vanilla essence and add to the sponge mixture. Stir gently. Leave to stand for 30 minutes.

Turn into a 1½ pint (900ml) well buttered pudding basin. Cover securely with buttered greaseproof paper and steam very gently for 1 hour.

When cooked, turn out carefully onto warmed plate, serve with fresh double cream.

BREAD AND BUTTER PUDDING

Serves 4

6 thin slices of white bread,
crusts removed
2 oz (50g) English butter
2 oz (50g) currants or sultanas
1½ oz (40g) castor sugar
2 eggs
1 pint (570ml) milk

Thickly spread bread slices with butter, cut into fingers or small squares. Put half into a 2 pint (1.1 litre) buttered ovenproof dish. Sprinkle with all the fruit and half the sugar. Top with the remaining bread, buttered side uppermost. Sprinkle with the rest of the sugar. Beat the eggs and milk well together. Strain into dish over bread. Leave to stand for 30 minutes so that the bread absorbs some of the liquid.

Bake in the oven at gas mark 3 (325°f) (170°c) for 45-60 minutes, until set and the top is crisp and golden.

THE IMPORTANCE OF BEING EARNEST
by **Oscar Wilde**
Lyttelton 16 September 1982,
Director **Peter Hall**
Algernon **Nigel Havers**, Jack **Martin Jarvis**, Lady Bracknell **Judi Dench,** Gwendolen **Zoë Wanamaker**, Lane **Brian Kent**

LADY BRACKNELL I'm sorry if we are a little late, Algernon, but I was obliged to call on dear Lady Harbury. I hadn't been there since her poor husband's death. I never saw a woman so altered; she looks quite twenty years younger. And now I'll have a cup of tea, and one of those nice cucumber sandwiches you promised me.

ALGERNON Certainly, Aunt Augusta. (Goes over to tea-table)

LADY BRACKNELL Won't you come and sit here, Gwendolen?

GWENDOLEN Thanks, mamma, I'm quite comfortable where I am.

ALGERNON (picking up empty plate in horror) Good heavens! Lane! Why are there no cucumber sandwiches? I ordered them specially.

LANE (gravely) There were no cucumbers in the market this morning, sir. I went down twice.

ALGERNON No cucumbers!

LANE No, sir. Not even for ready money.

RASPBERRY CROWDIE

Serves 4

2 oz (50g) medium oatmeal
10 fl oz (275ml) fresh double
cream
4 tablespoons clear honey
3 tablespoons whisky
12 oz (350g) fresh raspberries

Place the oatmeal in a tray and toast until golden brown. Leave to cool.

Whip the fresh cream until softly stiff, then stir in the honey, whisky and cooled oatmeal.

Pick over the raspberries, reserve a few for decoration. Layer up the raspberries and fresh cream mixture in four tall whisky tumblers. Cover with cling film and refrigerate.

Allow to come to room temperature for 10 minutes before serving. Decorate with the reserved raspberries.

LOVE'S LABOUR'S LOST
by **William Shakespeare**
Old Vic 19 December 1968,
Director **Laurence Olivier**
King of Navarre **Derek Jacobi**,
Costard **John McEnery**

KING Sir, I will pronounce your sentence: you shall fast a week with bran and water.

COSTARD I had rather pray a month with mutton and porridge.

TARTE TATIN

Serves 4

½ oz (10g) unsalted butter
3 oz (75g) soft brown sugar
1 lb (450g) dessert apples

For pastry

4 oz (125g) plain flour
2 oz (50g) unsalted butter
1 oz (25g) icing sugar
1 egg yolk
4 fl oz (125ml) crème fraîche

Melt the ½ oz of unsalted butter and brush over the inside of a shallow 8 inch (20.5cm) sponge tin. Line the base with greaseproof paper cut to fit, and brush with remaining melted butter. Sprinkle the brown sugar evenly over the paper. Place to one side.

Sift the flour into a basin, add the 2 oz (50g) of butter and rub into flour. Sift in the icing sugar and stir in the egg yolk and a tablespoon of water. Mix to a rough dough. Turn out onto a floured working surface and knead until smooth. Roll out the pastry to a circle the size of the tin and trim neatly. Set aside.

Peel, core and thickly slice the apples, arrange the slices over the brown sugar. Carefully place the pastry over the top of apple slices and press down gently. Bake in centre of oven at gas mark 4 (350°f) (180°c) for 35-40 minutes until crisp and golden brown.

Cool the tart for 5 minutes and turn out upside down onto serving plate. Remove the paper and serve the tart hot with crème fraîche.

CYRANO
by **Edmond Rostand**
adapted by **Patrick Garland**
Old Vic 27 October 1970,
Director **Patrick Garland**
Ragueneau **Gerald James**

RAGUENEAU That's not the way to make dough rise, your pastry's dull and stodgy and prosaic – it should be light and crusty, like one of the epigrams of Montaigne. Where's the metaphor in your blackcurrant pie, it's all similes, and the vol au vents need far more dainty alliteration – they should trip off the tongue – remember your Racine, mes amis, "Pour qui sont ses serpentes qui sifflent sur vos têtes". Ah, that's better, the game pie is as exquisite as a villanelle, and these éclairs a sequence of classical Alexandrine sonnets. You should follow the example of Monsieur Cyrano – there's a man who lives and dies by poetry – he'll give you a duel in verse. He'll kill you with a couplet.

FRUITCAKE

Serves 12

2 oz (50g) split almonds
3 oz (75g) self raising flour
8 oz (225g) plain flour
pinch of salt
pinch of mixed spice
8 oz (225g) unsalted butter
8 oz (225g) soft brown sugar
1 orange zest grated
1 lemon zest grated
4 large eggs
8 oz (225g) currants
8 oz (225g) sultanas
6 oz (175g) raisins
4 oz (125g) chopped mixed
peel
4 oz (125g) glacé cherries
chopped

Pre-heat the oven to gas mark 3 (325°f) (170°c), grease and line with greaseproof paper an 8 inch (20.5cm) square cake tin.

Blanch the almonds, chop half of them and set aside. Sieve the flour, salt and mixed spices together. Cream the butter and sugar, add the grated orange and lemon zest, then add the eggs one at a time, alternating with the flour mixture.

Mix the currants, sultanas, raisins, mixed peel and cherries, together with the chopped almonds, into the smooth mixture.

Place into the prepared tin, smooth the top and arrange the remaining split almonds neatly on top. Place the cake in pre-heated oven and bake for 3 hours.

POPPYSEED CAKE

Serves 6

For the pastry

5 oz (150g) ground poppy
seeds
6 fl oz (175 ml) milk
4 oz (125g) granulated sugar
2 oz (50g) plain chocolate
(grated)
2 oz (50g) seedless raisins
2 oz (50g) chopped candied
orange peel
2 oz (50g) grated blanched
almonds

For the glaze

1 teaspoon of beaten egg
castor sugar
whole poppy seeds

To make the pastry, cream the butter, sugar and salt. Add the egg, then flour and enough water to make a soft, but not sticky, dough. Chill for 1 hour. Roll out thinly and cut out four 8" (20cm) circles to fit into an 8" (20cm) loose-bottomed flat tin. Put one circle into the tin.

To make the filling, simmer the ground poppy seeds in the milk for 2 minutes, stirring. Remove from the heat and add the remaining ingredients, except for the teaspoon of the egg needed for the glaze. Set oven at moderate, gas mark 3 (170°c) (325°F). Spread one-third of the filling on the pastry circle in the tin. Cover with a second circle and another third of the filling, then with the third circle and the rest of the filling. Cover with the last circle and press the edge down very lightly. Make a central hole and brush the top with the teaspoon of egg. Sprinkle lightly with sugar and whole poppy seeds. Bake at the top of the heated oven for 45-60 minutes. Serve warm.

MRS KLEIN

by **Nicholas Wright**

Cottesloe 10 August 1988 (West End
from 6 December 1988),
Director **Peter Gill**
Mrs Klein **Gillian Barge,**
Paula **Zoë Wanamaker**

MRS KLEIN is sorting through
old papers. Paula is listening.

MRS KLEIN It's quite incredi-
ble what one keeps. (Tears up
a photograph. Finds a piece of
paper.) This is a poem he

wrote. (Reads it.) Excuse me.
(She cries. Holds her hand out.
Paula takes it. She slowly
stops crying.) I think that's it till
next time. So: our coffee
should be ready. You'll have
some?

PAULA Thank you.

MRS KLEIN Now what's this?

PAULA I've brought you
something.

(It's a cakebox)

MRS KLEIN But my dear you
shouldn't have spent your
money. No don't tell me. .
(Opens it) Paula, this is fantas-
tic of you. Poppy-seed cake,
no reason you should believe
this, was my mother's
speciality.

The Photographs

Authors' acknowledgements

Excerpts reprinted by kind permission of the following:

From Edward Albee's *Counting the Ways* – William Morris Agency (UK) Ltd

From Alan Ayckbourn's *Bedroom Farce* – Alan Ayckbourn

From Samuel Beckett's *Waiting for Godot* – Faber & Faber Ltd

From Alan Bennett's adaptation of Kenneth Grahame's *The Wind in the Willows* published by Faber & Faber Ltd – Alan Bennett; and from his *Single Spies* – Faber & Faber Ltd and Simon & Schuster

From Eric Bentley's translation of Bertolt Brecht's *Mother Courage* – Methuen London, Stefan Brecht and Eric Bentley

From Howard Brenton's *The Romans in Britain* – Methuen London

From Harold Brighouse's *Hobson's Choice* – Samuel French Ltd

From Moura Budberg's translation of Anton Chekhov's *Three Sisters* – Davis-Poynter Ltd

From Noël Coward's *Blithe Spirit* © 1941 The Estate of Noël Coward – Methuen London and Michael Imison Playwrights Ltd London

From Keith Dewhurst's *Lark Rise* (from Flora Thompson's book) – Stanley Thornes (Publishers) Ltd

From Brian Friel's *Dancing at Lughnasa* © Brian Friel – Faber & Faber Ltd and Curtis Brown, London, on behalf of Brian Friel

From Athol Fugard's *A Place with the Pigs* – Faber & Faber Ltd and William Morris Agency (UK) Ltd

From Patrick Garland's adaptation of Edmond Rostand's *Cyrano* – Curtis Brown, London, on behalf of Patrick Garland

From Trevor Griffiths' *Piano* – Faber & Faber Ltd

From Christopher Hampton's *White Chameleon* – Faber & Faber Ltd

From David Hare's *Wrecked Eggs, Racing Demon, Plenty, The Secret Rapture* and *Murmuring Judges* – David Hare and Faber & Faber Ltd

From Tony Harrison's version of Molière's *The Misanthrope* – Tony Harrison

From Lilian Hellman's *Watch on the Rhine* – Random House, New York

From Ronald Hingley's translation of Anton Chekhov's *The Cherry Orchard* – Ronald Hingley

From John Lennon's *In His Own Write* – Jonathan Cape and Shukat & Hafin

From C D Locock's translation of August Strindberg's *Dance of Death* – The Trustees of the Anglo-Swedish Literary Foundation

From Robert David MacDonald's translation of Bertolt Brecht's *The Threepenny Opera* – Robert David MacDonald and Universal Edition

From David Mamet's *American Buffalo* – Methuen London and William Morris Agency (UK) Ltd

From Adrian Mitchell's *The Pied Piper* – text published by Oberon Books Ltd; and from his version of Calderon's *The Mayor of Zalamea* – Absolute Classics

From Julian Mitchell's *Half-Life* – Julian Mitchell

From Daniel Mornin's *At Our Table* – Daniel Mornin

From John Mortimer's versions of Feydeau's *A Flea In Her Ear* and *The Lady from Maxim's*, published by Samuel French Ltd, and Zuckmayer's *The Captain of Köpenick*, published by Methuen London – John Mortimer

From Peter Nichols' *The National Health* – Faber & Faber Ltd and Grove Press, Inc

From J B Priestley's *When We Are Married*, published by Samuel French Ltd – The Estate of J B Priestley

From Terence Rattigan's *The Browning Version* © 1949 Executors and Trustees of the late Sir Terence Rattigan – Michael Imison Playwrights Ltd London

From Jeremy Sams' translation of Molière's *The Miser*. Translation © 1991 Jeremy Sams – Michael Imison Playwrights Ltd London

From Peter Shaffer's *Amadeus* – Peter Shaffer

From Neil Simon's *Brighton Beach Memoirs* © 1984 by Neil Simon – Neil Simon

From Tom Stoppard's *Jumpers* – Faber & Faber Ltd and Grove Press, Inc; and from his *Rough Crossing* (from Molnar) and *On the Razzle* (from Nestroy) – Faber & Faber Ltd and Tom Stoppard

From Peter Tinniswood's translation of Eduardo de Filippo's *Napoli Milionaria*. Original play © 1950 The Estate of Eduardo de Filippo – Michael Imison Playwrights Ltd London. Translation © 1991 Peter Tinniswood – Jonathan Clowes Ltd

From Richard Wilbur's translation of Molière's *Tartuffe* © 1963, 1962, 1961, and renewed 1989 by Richard Wilbur – Harcourt Brace Jovanovich, Inc.

From Tennessee Williams' *Cat on a Hot Tin Roof* – The Trustees of the Estate of Tennessee Williams

From August Wilson's *Ma Rainey's Black Bottom* (Penguin Books 1988) © 1985 by August Wilson – New American Library, a division of Penguin Books USA Inc and Penguin Books Ltd London

From Charles Wood's translation of Pirandello's *Man Beast and Virtue* – Absolute Classics, and from his *H* – William Morris Agency (UK) Ltd

From Nicholas Wright's *Mrs Klein* © Nicholas Wright 1988 – Nick Hern Books

INDEX OF RECIPES

Pork Tenderloin with Plum
Sauce 89
Pork Loin with Gin and Juniper
Berries 90
Veal Piccata with Mustard
Sauce 92
Blanquette of Veal 94
Medallions of Veal with Lemon
Sauce 96
Veal Steak with Sage and Parma
Ham 97
Steak with Stilton and Madeira
Sauce 98
Filet Mignon with Walnut
Sauce 101
Roast Quail with Black Olives and
Thyme 102
Pheasant Casserole 103
Pot Roasted Grouse with
Honey 104
Venison Pie 105
Rump Steak and Oyster Pie 106
Shepherd's Pie 107
Cassoulet 108

Sauces

Basic Velouté Sauce 21
Mayonnaise 21
Avocado Sauce 25
Béchamel Sauce 29
White Wine & Butter Sauce 30
Dill & Mustard Sauce 46
Watercress Sauce 48
Pesto Sauce 51
Tomato Coulis 55
Sorrel Sauce 69

Desserts

Pink Grapefruit and Vermouth
Sorbet 111
Apple, Apricot and Calvados
Mousse 112
Iced Capuccino Mousse 114
Pure Genius Mousse 115
Mango Fool 116
Raspberry Fool 117
Amaretto Syllabub 117
Lime Syllabub 118
Whisky Syllabub 118
Blackcurrant and Cassis Jelly 119
Peach Melba 120
Vanilla Poached Pear 121
Raspberry Bavarois 121
Marsala Sabayon Mousse 122
Almond Blancmange 123
Strawberry Romanoff 123
Gaelic Coffee Trifle 124
Snow Dumplings 125
Crème Brûlée 126
Summer Pudding with Chantilly
Cream 128
Queen of Puddings 129
Cherry Batter Pudding 130
Cabinet Pudding 131
Bread and Butter Pudding 132
Raspberry Crowdie 133
Tarte Tatin 134
Fruitcake 135
Poppyseed Cake 136